The Mysterious Jesus Message

We Would Never Have Known
Had Jesus Not Delivered the Message

Jim Fitch

Revelations of Grace, Joy, and Peace

Cover design: Joy L. Fitch
Cover photo: © GaryAlvis/iStockphoto

Foreword

We have seriously neglected a foundational part of the mission of Jesus. The Gospel of John mentions this subject over thirty times. It was obviously a key part of what Jesus was doing here among us: his message.

Jesus came to reveal truth about God, about us, and about how to live life. What he revealed constituted the content of his message to the world.

The reality of this fact had escaped me for forty years of serious Bible study. It was obscured by English words used to translate the Greek New Testament. Most often the English word "word" was used to translate the Greek word *logos*. In places this is a good translation. Most of the time it should have been translated as message or communication and occasionally as revelation.

Using word in our translations hid the idea of Jesus delivering a message from God to us. When we break through this habit and see what is really there in the Greek New Testament we begin to understand the power of what Jesus was doing.

Jesus taught many radically new concepts about God and life. Even more powerfully, he lived out his message. He did not just tell us about God and who he is. He demonstrated the spirit and lifestyle of God through his own spirit and lifestyle. He revealed the Father by means of his own person.

His message is all about truth and falsity. He told those Judeans following him in John 8 that they had been lied to all of their lives about God and his ways. He said that he had come to tell them the truth and set them free from the misunderstandings and misbeliefs that controlled their thinking and living.

His message is a message of truth. He said in John 5.24-25 that those who believe his message can have the life of God, the life of eternity, eternal life. What a powerful statement. The truths he has delivered have the power to change people and their lives, to actually give life.

If this is true, we must discover those spirit-changing and life-changing truths. Exactly what are those truths that are so different than what we normally believe? What did Jesus teach and demonstrate that is so powerful?

This book is the result of my journey to answer those questions. I admit that it is a feeble attempt to convey the discoveries that I made. But, it is a beginning to pull back the veil to some of the mysteries about God and the heavens.

I pray that you are challenged and touched by what is here.

Jim Fitch
Brentwood 2012

Contents

Book One: The Life Giving Power of the Jesus Message

Book Two: The Details of the Jesus Message

Part One: Characteristics of the Jesus Message

Part Two: Foundations of the Jesus Message

Part Three: Content of the Jesus Message

Introduction

The content of this book is different than the normal book about Jesus. It embodies a different viewpoint and understanding of what he was doing with his life and ministry. The differences were not intentional. I am a life long evangelical Christian who was nurtured in the traditional understandings of that movement. But something happened along the way during forty years of biblical studies. My understandings of the message of the New Testament changed from the traditional. The change was purely unintentional.

Several convictions about the New Testament and its study influenced the outcomes I have come to believe.

First, I have believed that the New Testament was intended by God and the individual writers to be understood by its readers. I have never subscribed to the idea that we are not supposed to understand, just accept. The writers were people like us and they were writing to people like us. What they wrote had clear meaning to themselves and they hoped it would to those who received it. Our task is to discover their original meanings.

Discovering original meanings is not an easy task. Two thousand years and several different languages involved make the task difficult. The writings were set in the cultures of the Mediterranean and the Middle East, and those cultures can be a puzzle for us in the twenty-first century West.

The Bible is a collection of words and concepts. Those words were written originally in Hebrew, Aramaic, and Greek. They reflected mindsets, symbolisms, and idioms of their day, and many are puzzling to us today.

I am convinced that God wants us to understand the message of those words to us, and to be informed and touched by their meanings.

Second, I have believed that the most accurate Bible study is that which allows the biblical text to be what it is and say what it intends to say. It may be impossible to approach the text without preconceived understandings of what it is attempting to say, but we must discipline ourselves to do just that. We must seek out what the original writer meant by his writing, not what our theology or philosophical construct dictates about it. We must allow the writer to speak his thoughts and his information to us. We cannot box him in with our preconceptions.

Third, I have believed that the Bible is what it is. It is not what we would like for it to be, or what we need for it to be. It is what it is whether we like it or not. Many theologians have tried to make the Bible to be what they need for it to be for their own practical or philosophical reasons. Some religious politicians have used the Bible to help them achieve their own ends, as politicians are want to do. It has often been just another tool in their quest to achieve their goals. The Roman emperor Constantine is a good example of this problem. He needed a state religion to hold his fragile empire together. He fashioned Christianity into a state religion to accomplish that purpose. It became his political tool.

Some theological philosophers have used the Bible to make sense within their philosophical constructs. They have required that it be understood in certain ways to help their conclusions to be reasonable. They have difficulty letting it be what it is.

None of these groups can make the Bible be what it is not. They can do their best to convince us that it is something that it is not, but we always have nagging suspicions that something is out of sync with the truth. As Shakespeare said, "The truth will out". It never goes away. It is always hanging around waiting to be discovered.

Fourth, I have believed that the biblical message is reasonable and orderly. Everything that God has created appears to be reasonable and orderly. This fact has allowed scientists to go about their business with the confidence that chaos is not controlling the understandings they pursue.

The Bible is just as reasonable and orderly. It is not filled with unreasonable inconsistencies. It may contain inconsistencies and disagreements, but they are what they are for good reasons. Our task is to understand those reasons and allow them to be what they are.

This fourth point has been a "deal breaker" in my personal quest to understand the biblical message. Many traditional interpretations and expositions of the New Testament have been riddled with unreasonable conclusions. Many have forced the original texts into philosophical molds that violate the original meanings of those texts.

I have been plagued from an early age by these inconsistencies in the Christian belief system that I was being taught. Many conclusions did not ring true to me as I studied the Bible. I began to perceive that many scholars were forcing their interpretations into texts rather than allowing those texts to speak their intended message. They were using the New Testament for their own understandings and purposes rather than allowing it to speak its own. This conclusion started my quest to question established understandings and search for others more consistent with original biblical intentions.

The search for understanding has led to conclusions that I never foresaw. I never dreamed that the text was saying what I have come to believe that it says.

Some of my conclusions are different than the orthodox, but they are based on New Testament content. I think they are true to the biblical message. I have not sought to make the Bible say anything. I have sought to let it speak its intended message. I have simply wanted to understand what God and his writers are saying.

Be aware that some of my understandings of words and concepts are very different than the traditional. They will not make sense to the reader if understood in old ways.

The search for reasonableness and consistency has been a long one with some dead ends along the way. But what is reflected in this book, I believe to be reasonable and consistent with the New Testament.

Open your mind, soften your heart, and enjoy a new adventure in faith in Jesus Christ.

Translation of New Testament Verses

The translation of the New Testament passages presented here are those of the author. It comes from a lifetime of struggling to understand the meaning of key Greek words in the original manuscripts. It reflects my conclusions about those meanings.

The results attempt to be a translation, not a paraphrase. Word for word translations are never the standard for those translating from one language to another. Too many words cannot be translated by one single word in another language. Words do not always match up from language to language.

Translating meanings from one language to another sometimes requires multiple words to translate one word. This is true of the New Testament and is reflected in our translation.

Key words used by the young Christian movement are pivotal in understanding its message and that of Jesus. Some of these words have been skewed by historic translators in favor of their beliefs or theology. Some have been Anglicized or transliterated instead of being translated. We attempt to recapture original meanings of these key words. The message does not communicate if its words are unclear or misleading.

These key words are our favorite and most used words in the Christian world. Our translation will change some that may be held dear by you. Bear with us and discover why we have changed their traditional definitions. They may be strange at first, but they convey important parts of the message of Jesus to us, and we must make that message as clear as possible.

Jesus was all about words. He was communicating his revelations to us with words. If we miss the meanings of those words, we miss the power of the message.

Thankfully, Jesus also communicated his message about God, his spirit, and his lifestyle to us by means of his own spirit and lifestyle as well as his words. Observing Jesus helps us know more about how he was using the words he spoke. He lived his message as well as spoke his message.

Messengers and Messages

God has been sending messengers to humanity throughout recorded history. They have been called angels, which means "messengers," prophets, those who speak for God, and teachers. The Hebrew Old Testament is filled with instances when angels visited persons, and prophets held forth with their messages from God.

These messengers arose or appeared at crucial times in the lives of persons and societies. They gave direction, information, interpretation, and promises to the peoples to whom they appeared. They identified their messages as being from God himself.

Messages from God have given direction to the future of whole races and nations. Religions have been born because of them. Some of these messages have been preserved and revered as sacred, holy, and infallible. They have become the guiding lights for generations of peoples.

Abraham heard the voice of God and traveled to a new land and gave birth to the Jewish race. Moses followed and received his messages from God on a mountaintop, and they created the religious understandings and practices of the Jewish people.

Buddha and Confucius received understandings about life that birthed religions carrying their names. Mohammed got his messages from an angel of God and Islam was born. Joseph Smith was visited by the angel Moroni and Mormonism came into being.

Most of these leaders understood the messages that they had received as being from God, and they shared the messages with their world. People believed their messages, and believed them to be messengers from God to mankind.

Individuals continue to experience these kinds of personal revelations from God. For most, they are related to some aspect of their lives and remain personal for themselves. But the phenomenon of God speaking in some way to persons goes on. Messengers and messages are a normal part of the spiritual experiences of persons all over the world.

The concepts of messenger and message were also a central part of the mission and ministry of Jesus Christ. The awesome part of the message of Jesus is that it has the power to give a different kind of life to persons. When it is understood and believed, it can bring about changes in personalities and lifestyles. Not just any changes, but changes that lead to an overflow of wonder and joy. His message has a power to create a wondrous new kind of people on the Earth.

Why Have We Neglected The Jesus Message?

Some of the key teachings of Jesus about the personality of God have been obscured by long histories of misunderstood emphases and words. Disagreements about how to understand Jesus and his message started early in the Christian movement. Paul reflected these disagreements in his writings to the Galatians, Corinthians and Timothy. He spoke of "another gospel' than his. There were other people interpreting Jesus and his mission in different ways than his.

Institutional religion

In addition, as the decades passed, the movement became more and more molded into the forms of religion in its Mediterranean world. By the time it became the official religion of the Roman Empire in the 300s, Christianity was being forced into a state religion mold. The movement which led to finding the truth about God and life began to take the shape of all other religions with priests, temples, authoritarian hierarchies, observances and ceremonies. Its emphasis on truth and new life was lost to new emphases on traditional elements of state religion.

The needs of a state religion determined the parts of the new faith that were valued. The original emphasis on beliefs, life, and lifestyle were displaced by religious mystery. The original intent of Jesus was obscured by religious trappings. The original intent became secret. It became hidden from the world in favor of religious stuff.

Skewed word meanings

The second factor that caused neglect of the message was the misunderstanding of key words used by the faith. Words are intended to convey meaning from persons to persons. When the definition of key words are obscured or changed, the meanings of those words are lost. Their original message becomes hidden.

Key words used by Jesus suffered this fate. Words like grace, *agape*, sin, life, spirit, and eternal have been skewed by theologians to fit philosophical systems developed to interpret Christianity to the world. In addition, acceptable translations of these words into English have often been controlled by church authorities. Simple concepts easily understandable to all have been made to be difficult theological exercises. The original intent has become hidden, a secret.

We will attempt to rescue these New Testament concepts and words from their hidden prisons. In so doing, we will reassert the Jesus emphasis on new and overflowing life in the here and now. We will explore the joy that is hidden in the English biblical text by super serious translators. We will try to find the truths that Jesus said could set us free to live.

Book One: The Life Giving Power of the Jesus Message

The Birth from Above

Jesus answered him, "Truly I say to you, unless a person has been born from above, he cannot experience the Kingdom of God."

Nicodemus said to him, "How can a man be born while old? Can he enter his mother's womb a second time and be born?"

Jesus answered, "Truly I say to you, unless a person is born of water and of spirit he is not able to enter the Kingdom of God. That which has been born of the flesh is flesh; and that which is born of the spirit is spirit. (John 3.3-6)

With these words, Jesus Christ introduced a new phenomenon to the world. He insisted that every person needs to be reborn in spirit. The natural condition of us all is less than God intends and desires for us. We need to change and become like he wants us to become.

Historically, these verses have been understood to relate to morality and to the end of life when we can enter into heaven. This understanding has prevailed in spite of the many references by Jesus and New Testament writers to a creation of new life in persons in the here and now. Jesus actually emphasized a change in spirit and life now rather than later. God wants us to be different kinds of persons now. When that happens, later takes care of itself.

The New Testament is all about this experience of new life. From beginning to end it shares experiences about being spiritually remade.

Jesus used the phrase, "born from above" to identify the source of this new life. It is life that is from the Living God. It is heavenly life. It is life like that of God himself. It is "eternal" life, or as the Greek reads, "life of the ages of the ages" or "life of the eons of the eons".

Jesus reveals to us that God wants us to be like him. That God wants us to have his Spirit, attitude, values, behavior, and lifestyle. God wants to put his Spirit into us. When we are born of his Spirit we begin to become like him in all aspects of our living. And those aspects are wonderful.

Jesus said that we are not spiritually alive

Jesus said to him, "Follow me; and let the dead bury their dead." (Matt. 8:22)

Jesus said to her, "I am the coming to life, and the life: he who believes in me, although he was dead, yet he shall live:" (John 11:25)

Jesus used the metaphor of life and death to illustrate the effects of his teachings about belief and living. The concepts behind these words have been a puzzle to the Christian world from its earliest days. It finally attributed his sayings to the end of life rather than to present living. The life he promised must refer to everlasting life after death, and the death he spoke of must mean spiritual death after this life is over.

The problem with that understanding is that Jesus gives every indication that he is speaking of the here and now, not the hereafter.

We know that we have passed from death into life, because we are gracious to the brethren. He who is not gracious to his brother is living in death. (1 John 3:14)

Jesus speaks of a mindset and lifestyle that gives life to persons, as over against mindsets and lifestyles which doom and destroy spirit and life. This is an illusive line that he draws. But he often proclaims understandings and behavior that he says will fill life to the fullest, even to overflowing. (John 10:10)

He contrasts his teachings to wrong beliefs and behavior that rob life of its fullness, honor, dignity, and peace. He notes that we have been killed by lies about life.

"You are from a diabolic father, and the passions of your father you want to pursue. He was a killer from the beginning, and did not stand for truth, because truth is not in him. Whenever he speaks falsely, he speaks from himself, because he is a liar and the father of liars. Because I speak the truth, you do not believe me." (John 8:44-45)

Jesus said to him, "I am the way, the truth, and the life..." (John 14:6)

Jesus came so that we could have this new life and not remain "dead". He often talked about the experience of coming to life and the means for having this experience.

The message of life

"Make them godly by means of the truth; your message is truth." (Jesus to God, John 17.17)

In keeping with his will, he birthed us again by the message of truth, so that we would be a kind of first edition among his creations. (James 1.18)

"It is the spirit that gives life. The flesh profits nothing. The words that I speak to you, they are spirit, and they are life." (Jesus in John 6:63)

The experience of new spirit and life comes through the means of the revelations and teachings of Jesus. He has revealed the person and spirit of God, the truth about us, and the truth about how to live life. In so doing, he has begun the process for a new spiritual birth in each of us.

Jesus delivered his message in two ways: he taught his message and he lived his message. The second way is very important because Jesus demonstrated the spirit of God in his own personality even more powerfully than he taught it in his teachings. He was a living example of the spirit and personality of the Father.

That demonstration of personality and behavior is far more powerful than simply teaching about them. But, the truth of this happening forces us to work to discover what kind of personality Jesus had that was so revelatory. What was so different about his personality and spirit?

And, what did Jesus mean by spirit?

Jesus used the Greek word *pneuma* to identify that part of us which is called our spirits. It is the invisible part of us that controls who we are as persons. The body simply reflects the characteristics of our spirits. Note the John 6.63 verse above. Our bodies are not in control of who we are. Our spirits control us. Jesus uses the word in much the same way as we use the word personality. It is the force of life within us that expresses itself in our attitudes and behaviors.

The ancients believed that we are composed of two entities: body and spirit. We have a body and we have a spirit or spirits that reside in that body. Our bodies are controlled and directed by our spirits. Life in us is in the spirit. When the spirit leaves our bodies, the bodies die.

The gospels contain many stories about Jesus and the spirits of persons. He cast out demonic and unclean spirits from people. These spirits were causing great harm to the persons whom they possessed.

We use spirit in a similar way when we say that persons are possessed by spirits of greed, hatefulness, or an unforgiving spirit. These spirits are observable and identifiable in the lives of persons.

Changing spirits

Interestingly, Jesus said that our spirits can be changed. That is what this idea of rebirth is all about. Our spirits need to be redone. As products of our normal world, our spirits contain many detrimental and life depleting characteristics. They are oriented in ways that kill our lives. Jesus said that he came to change that life killing part of us.

On one occasion, he talked about casting out undesirable spirits in a way that could be detrimental to ourselves. He told the parable of a bad spirit being cast our of a life, but the life was not filled with some better spirit and the old spirit came back and brought others with it which were worse then itself. The teaching being that getting rid of bad spirits is not sufficient. Our lives must be filled with the right kind of spirit in order for undesirable spirits to be kept out.

"The unclean spirit when it has gone out of the man, journeys through waterless places, seeking rest, and finding none, it says, 'I will return to my house from which I came out.' When it returns, it discovers it swept and cleaned. So it goes, and takes with it seven other spirits worse than itself. They enter in and live there. The last state of that man has become worse than the first." (Jesus in Luke 11.24-26)

Jesus said that he had come to help us to have a rebirth of our spirit so that we may be possessed by a spirit like that of God. The Spirit of God is a life-giving spirit that causes our lives to overflow with that which is good and wonderful in life.

When the New Testament speaks about spiritual things it is not simply referring to things in the heavenly world. It is speaking of that which relates to our spirits. This is in contrast to that which speaks to our physical side. Jesus came to rebirth our spirits. He was all about the "spiritual".

The Spirit from Above

Jesus told Nicodemus that he needed to be born from above. This vignette continues the emphasis of John on this new birth of the spirit that is the central theme of his book. He had begun with the testimony of John the Baptist that he had seen the spirit coming down from heaven like a dove.

John bore witness saying, "I have seen the Spirit coming down like a dove out of heaven, and it lived in him. I did not know him, but the one who sent me to immerse in water, he said to me, 'Upon the one whom you see the Spirit descending and living in him, it is he who immerses in the Spirit of God.' I have seen, and have borne witness that this is the Son of God." (John about Jesus 1.32-34)

This phenomenon of the Spirit coming down was experienced in a variety of settings in the New Testament. When it fell on people it had very observable effects. They became a very different kind of people.

While they were praying, the room was shaken where they were assembled together; and they were all filled with the Holy Spirit, and they shared the message of God with great courage. (Acts 4:31)

To the surprise of Peter, the Spirit could come into the life of anyone, even a Gentile. He saw it happen to the people of Antioch in Syria.

"As I began to speak, the Holy Spirit fell on them, even as it did on us in the beginning. I remembered the message of the Lord, how he said, 'John surely immersed in water; but you shall be immersed in the Holy Spirit.' If then, God gave to them the same gift as he did to us when we believed in the Lord Jesus Christ, who was I that I could resist God?" (Acts 11.15-17)

When we discuss the spirit from above, we come quickly to the question of how this spirit may be different than any other. Since the Baptist identified it as the Spirit of God, an additional question arises. Of all of the possible kinds of spirits that exist, what are the characteristics of the Spirit of God? It was obviously identifiable and observable in its effects on persons. People could see the results of its presence in certain people.

Therefore, brethren, seek out from among you seven men with good reputations, full of the Spirit, and of wisdom, to whom we may assign this business. (Acts 6.3)

The early church leaders could see the presence of the Spirit in persons. They could identify that some were more full of it than others. The presence of the Spirit in their lives was obvious.

John experienced the same situation and he reflected it in his instructions to the young churches. He said for them to "test" the spirits of those who claimed to be speaking for God when they came to them.

Gracious brothers, do not trust every spirit, but test the spirits to see if they are of God. Because many false prophets are out and about in the world. (1 John 4.1)

The spirits of these self proclaimed prophets of God could be observed and evaluated. John cautioned the churches to be discriminating in whom they listened to as spokesmen for God. He continued on in that fourth chapter to define the kind of spirit that is characteristic of God. He used the Greek word *agape* extensively in the chapter as the key word to identify the spirit that is of God. If these prophets did not demonstrate *agape* in their spirits and behavior, they did not understand who God really is or what he is about.

A spirit of grace and *agape*

The New Testament uses two key words to identify the spirit and personality of God. They are difficult for us to translate into English because we do not have exactly the same words in our language. Translators have made peace with the use of a couple of English words, but they are deficient of some of the important meanings of the original Greek words.

The Greek word *charis* (caris) is normally translated as "grace" in English. Grace has some of the meaning of *charis* but not all. It does well in conveying the idea of a gift or gifting behavior, but an additional element is missing.

Charis is part of a family of Greek words that are very similar in meaning.

Chara (cara) is usually translated into English as "joy" or "happiness".

Charin (carin) is usually translated as "favor".

Charisma (carisma) is translated as "gift".

The gift part of the meaning of *charis* is familiar to us. The joy or happy part of the word usually escapes us. These words convey a sense of a happy gift or a gift of joy.

Jesus demonstrated this happy gift idea in both his spirit and behavior. He was constantly giving people undeserved gifts which resulted in happiness for them. Whether he was healing, casting out demons, feeding hungry people, making wine out of water, or refusing to stone sinners, he was always giving gifts of joy to people. He was a man of grace who had a spirit and lifestyle of grace. He spread gifts of joy around to everyone. John noted this at the very beginning of his book:

From his overflow we have all received: happy gift [grace] after happy gift. (John 1.16)

Jesus taught a gift-giving lifestyle

Jesus' lifestyle teachings conveyed the same spirit of grace. He rejected legalistic judgmentalism and its harsh spirit and behavior. He taught gifting, happy ways to behave.

We are to freely give a second mile.
We are to give a cloak as well as a coat.
We are to pray for persecutors.
We are to return good for bad.
We are to overcome bad with good.
We are to forgive seventy times seven.

All of these instructions are behavior that gifts persons with a measure of happiness. Jesus said that when we are living out this spirit and behavior of gifting joy we are being like the Father:

"You have heard that it has been said, 'You shall be gracious to your neighbor, and hate your enemy.' But I say to you, 'Be gracious to your enemies, and pray for those who cause you problems'; so that you may be sons of your Father who is in heaven. He causes his sun to rise on the bad as well as the good, and sends rain on the just and the unjust." (Jesus in Matthew 5.43-45)

The spirit of happy gifting is the very opposite of being a person of legalistic rewards. Legalism instructs us to be persons of judgment who treat others as they deserve to be treated. If a person deserves our rebuke we rebuke them. If they deserve a blessing, we bless them. We give them that which they deserve. To be effective in living this way, we must develop the ability to measure people according to the rules and reward them accordingly.

Being a person of grace means that we have a spirit and lifestyle of gifting people who may not deserve any gift from us. We do not relate to them as they deserve from us, but we gift them with a blessing instead. That becomes who we are. We gift everyone whether they deserve a gift or not. We have God's spirit of joy in us and we share that joy with those around us. That is just what we do.

Because the Father is a person of joyful gifting we become people of joyful gifting. We have his Spirit in us. We become his spiritual offspring. We have his spiritual DNA. We increasingly become people of grace.

Grow in grace, and in the wisdom of our Lord and Savior Jesus Christ. Glory to him now and forever. Amen. (2 Peter 3.18)

Agape is awesome

The Greek word *agape* is very similar to *charis*. It has been a mystery word for English translators throughout history. Even though they know that the word for love in Greek is *phileo*, they have translated *agape* as love also. The two words obviously have different meanings, but the meaning of *agape* has been a puzzle for translators.

Groups often give words shades of meaning that are known to themselves but may be somewhat different than the use of the population as a whole. To discover these meanings, we must see how words were used in the context of the groups using them. This is what we must do with *agape*. The early Christians used the word in specific ways that are detectible when we search their writings.

Agape is arguably the single most important word in the New Testament. It is the key word in the Great Commandments of Jesus, and it is the defining word about God in 1 John 4: *God is agape*.

One process to use to discover its shades of meaning for Jesus is to begin with the second Great Commandment, to *agape* a neighbor.

Jesus gave many teachings about how to behave toward the people in our lives. He taught *agape* actions and demonstrated those actions in his own life. When we review some of them, they become very similar to those we have already considered. Jesus taught us to:

Forgive seventy times seven.
Overcome bad with good.
Never return bad for bad, but return good for bad.
And the list goes on.

These are the same behaviors we discussed above as examples of grace. If they are examples of *agape* to a neighbor, and they appear to be, they are the same as doing grace to a neighbor. This being true, grace and *agape* are words that define a very similar spirit and behavior. We may say that *agape* is grace in action. It is the doing of grace. It is doing happy gifting to others. What a powerful lifestyle!

When John says that God is *agape*, he is saying that he is a God who behaves toward the world in ways that are happy gifts. He delights in blessing us with good gifts. It puts in context the unusual statement of James about gifts from above.

Every good and filling gift is from above, and comes down from the Father of lights, who does not change nor turn. (James 1.17)

We can see how the spirit of a person can be "tested" if we understand the criteria of the test. John is speaking of an examination of a prophet's spirit to see if he has a spirit of gifting joy toward people. If he does not, then he is not speaking for God.

Early church leaders could be seen to be full of the Spirit of God if they were full of joyous gifting. If they were not, they were not full of the Spirit of God.

Paul describes God's spirit

The Apostle Paul wrote often about the presence of the Spirit of God in believers. He was not ambiguous about the characteristics of that spirit and described them with terms that are very observable in persons.

The product of the Spirit is graciousness, joy, peace, patience, kindness, goodness, faithfulness, gentleness, self-control; there is no law that can produce this kind of behavior.

Now those who belong to Christ Jesus have crucified the flesh with its passions and desires. If we live by the Spirit, let us also behave consistent with the Spirit. (Galatians 5.22-25)

This list of descriptors is stunning at first reading. The spirit and personality of God the Father is unlike that which is normally attributed to any god. When persons have been immersed in the Spirit of God they become

a giver of good gifts rather than being legalistic,

happy rather than unhappy,

peaceful rather than antagonistic,

patient rather than impatient,

kind rather than critical,

good rather than immoral,

dependable rather than untrustworthy,

gentle rather than harsh,

and in control of themselves rather than being ruled by passion.

This list is lengthy, but it is not at all exhaustive. It does not include other teachings of Jesus about forgiving, peacemaking, and being non judgmental, among other behavior. But Paul makes his point about a particular spirit and lifestyle. He paints a portrait of a wonderful kind of people.

Paul talks often of persons being the abode of the Spirit of God. The spirit comes to live in them, and begins to remake them to be like the Father and the Son.

Therefore, if anyone is in Christ, he is a new creation; the old things have passed away; behold, everything has become new. (2 Corinthians 5:17)

The Spirit of God, the spirit of joyous giving, creates new people by changing their spirits to be spirits of joyous giving. Persons who are angry, selfish, judgmental, greedy, immoral, and money grabbers, begin to become different than they have been. Their spirits and then their lifestyles begin to be patterned after Jesus and the Father.

Truly, I say to you, the time is coming and is here now, when the dead will hear the voice of the Son of God, and those responding shall have life. The kind of life the Father has in himself, he also gave the son that kind of life to have in himself." (John 5.25-26)

We are his creation, crafted in Christ Jesus for a good lifestyle, which God prepared beforehand so that we could live accordingly. (Ephesians 2.10)

Receiving the Spirit of God

How does one receive this spirit from above? How do we begin the process of becoming born from above? Jesus spoke of this often. He talked about being a communicator and communication from God, and that through his message life could be experienced.

Truly, I say to you, he who hears my message, and believes [God] sent me, has life of the heavens, and has no need to be condemned, but has passed out of death into life. Truly, I say to you, the hour is coming, and now is, when the dead shall hear and understand the sayings of the Son of God: and they who receive them shall become alive. For the kind of life the Father has in himself, he also gave the Son that kind of life to have in himself. (John 5:24-26)

The process of rebirth begins with hearing the message of Jesus. If we do not know about the revelations and teachings of Jesus, we cannot respond to them with belief. If we do not believe, we do not receive. It begins with hearing and accepting.

Peter shared the story of Jesus with those Gentiles in Antioch and as he was sharing, the spirit came into their lives. See Acts 11.15 above. They heard the story and things began to happen to them.

How then can they call on him in whom they have not believed? How can they believe in him of whom they have not heard? How can they hear without a proclaimer? (Romans 10.14)

But exactly what is this message that is being proclaimed? What are the specific revelations of Jesus that are so different and powerful? What is it that we can believe that can remake our spirits to be like his?

Jesus' demonstration of God

The first subject which he revealed was the spirit and personality of God himself. He indicated that we have completely misunderstood who God is and how he relates to us. He demonstrated the true spirit and behavior of the Father by means of his own spirit and behavior. Jesus and the New Testament writers spoke to this truth often.

Jesus told his disciples that he was a living demonstration of who God is. His spirit, actions, and attitudes were those of the heavenly Father.

Philip said to him, "Lord, show us the Father, and it will satisfy us."
*Jesus said to him, "Have I been with you such a long time, Philip, and you still do not understand me? **He who has seen me has seen the Father.** How can you still say, 'Show us the Father?'"* (John 14.8-9)

The testimony of John the Baptist that he had seen the Spirit of God coming down into Jesus was part of this same message. He was affirming that the spirit of Jesus was the same as that of God. Although detractors denied that God could be like Jesus, John was validating that he was exactly like God in spirit, and therefore, behavior.

The use of the designation "Son of God" carries this same idea. Jesus is the spiritual offspring of God. His spirit is like that of God because he is the spiritual offspring, son, of God. This name of Jesus was repeated often to defend his revelation that God is indeed like him in personality and behavior.

Later writers underscored this same truth in their proclamations. The writer of the Book of Hebrews pointedly began the book with such a statement.

*God, having in times past spoken to our ancestors through the prophets, in various fragments and by various means, has in these last days spoken to us in his Son, whom he appointed the receiver of all things, through whom also he made the age; **who being the reflection of his glory, and the very image of his character,** and under girding all these things with his powerful message, when he had cleansed us from 'missing the mark', sat down on the right hand of the Majesty on high. Having become so much better than other messengers, so that he has received a name more excellent than they.* (Hebrews 1.1-4)

This truth that Jesus was a living demonstration of the spirit and behavior of God was hugely significant to the gospel writers. If it were true, our understanding of God has to change radically. Jesus was nothing like the God proclaimed by the Pharisees, scribes, and religious lawyers of the day. They considered his claim to be blasphemy.

The Judeans picked up stones again in order to stone him. Jesus responded to them, "I have shown you many good behaviors from the Father. For which of these actions do you wish to stone me?"

The Judeans answered him, "We do not stone you for your good behavior, but for blasphemy; because you, being a man, make yourself God."

Jesus answered them, "Is it not written in your law, 'I said, ye are gods?' If he called them gods to whom the message of God came, and those writings cannot be discounted, how can you say about him whom the Father sanctified and sent into the world, 'You blaspheme', because I said, 'I am the Son of God?' If I am not behaving like my Father, do not believe me. But if I act like him, though you do not believe me, believe the actions so that you may know and understand that the Father is in me, and I am in the Father." (John 10.31-38)

Therefore, because of this, the Judeans tried even more to kill him, because he not only broke the Sabbath laws, but also called God his own Father, making himself like God. (John 5.18)

Jesus violated the religious laws and taboos of his day. He refused to punish immoral people like adulteresses. He paid no attention to labels on people whether they were religious, national, gender, or racial. He socialized with religious and social outcasts.

He behaved in ways and with attitudes that no one had ever identified with God. His personality and behavior were almost the exact opposite to that which all religions understood God to have.

Obscuring happiness and joy

The happiness of Jesus' personality has been effectively glossed over in English translations of the New Testament. Whether on purpose or by misunderstanding, the joy that characterized the life of Jesus does not stand out in the English text. It is beautifully evident in the original Greek text.

The hiding of the joy of Jesus is chiefly done by the English words chosen to translate key Greek words. Joy and happiness is there everywhere in the Greek, but not so much in English.

Words like grace, love, blessed, and abundance are good words, but they are devoid of the emotion of joy that the underlying Greek words possess. Grace means happy gift. Love is actually a translation of *agape* which also means to give happy gifts. Blessed actually means happy. Abundance actually paints a picture of an overflowing container. All of these words convey feelings of happiness and joy in Greek, but they get lost in our understandings of the English words.

Jesus appears to have been a happy and joyous person who loved to share that joy with everyone around him. His teachings about how to live life are best understood when they are seen to be accomplished by people with happy hearts. Happy people are more likely to act like Jesus. They find it easier to be patient, forgiving, gifting, and caring. Those behaviors are natural actions of a happy heart overflowing onto other people. Remember that Jesus was said to overflow.

From his overflow we have all received: happy gift [grace] after happy gift. (John 1.16)

The Judeans could not believe that God was like Jesus in personality and lifestyle. For him to say that God was like himself was dishonoring to God in their minds. God could not be like Jesus. If he were, all of the legalism of their worldview and theological system came tumbling down. The Temple and its sacrificial system would be unnecessary. The Judeans could never agree to this reality. God could not be like Jesus or Jesus like God. He could not be the spiritual offspring of God. They would not believe him.

Jesus declared that his revelation of God is true and accurate. To accurately know God, we have to believe what Jesus has revealed about him.

Jesus said to him, "I am the way, and the truth, and the life. No one comes to [know] the Father, if not through me. If you have known me, you have known my Father also. From now on you know him, and have seen him." (John 14.6-7)

Jesus' teachings about the personality of God

Jesus demonstrated the spirit and personality of God through his own spirit and lifestyle, and he also taught about him. He told parables that showed the spirit and behavior of God as he portrayed God as various persons in real life situations.

The Parable of the Prodigal Son shows God to be a loving father who is patient, loving, and forgiving to wayward people. He portrays a father who is so overjoyed with the return of his child that he throws a party to celebrate. He is a father who knows joy and knows how to celebrate.

The Parable of the Generous Employer shows God to be gifting to those who have not earned the gifts that he gives. He pays his workers the same whether they worked all day or only a part of the day. His pay is not connected to their deservedness. It is a gift from a person who loves to give gifts that cause joy and celebration in those receiving them. He is a gracious employer who practices *agape*.

The Parable of the Good Shepherd shows God to be seeking to find and rescue every last one of us. It portrays us as sheep who cannot always fend for ourselves in life. We need his guidance and protection and he pursues us to provide that which we need most. The emphasis is on the needs of the sheep more than on what they deserve. That a sheep has gotten itself lost is accepted. That the shepherd will not allow that to be the final word is indicative of the spirit and personality of God.

Jesus constantly demonstrated and taught a God whom the world has not known. The angry, legalistic, and judging gods of the pagans and Pharisees is not the living God of the universe. Jesus reveals him to be completely different than they thought him to be.

This revelation was completely and profoundly different than any understanding from the past. A happy, gracious, forgiving God of joy is the last kind of God any religion has ever thought to be real. The world has known God to be lawgiver, judge, and punisher. He is a god of earthquakes, disasters, floods, famines, diseases, and other punishments to sinful mankind. He has been a legalistic judge who dispenses rewards as they have been earned by people, both good and bad.

Jesus was a true religious revolutionary. He revealed God to be a loving Father who delights in giving humans gifts that are undeserved. He delights in joy and happiness. He is showering us with gifts constantly and we usually do not recognize them because we do not expect them. We expect his anger because we are acutely aware of our shortcomings and mistakes.

And he wants to put his spirit in us so that we can become like him. He wants us to be born from above.

Jesus' Life-Giving Message about God

How could the revelations of Jesus about God make a difference in us? How can they help us move from death to life? Ah, but they do.

What we believe about the person and behavior of God toward us and the world has great influence on our psyches and lifestyles. What we believe may cause us to live in fear or without fear. It may cause us to be critical and judging, or it may cause us to be caring and accepting. It may cause us to be filled with guilt or filled with peace. What we believe about God and his spirit controls the kind of spirit that is in us.

The keys are truth and belief. If we believe that Jesus has revealed the truth about God to us, we begin to experience the results of that belief. If we really believe that God is a God of happiness, joy, and constant gifts to us, we begin to have that same spirit in ourselves. We begin to become people of happiness, joy, and gracious gifts. It is almost a magical phenomenon. Our beliefs begin to give us a quality of spirit and life that we have not known before. We begin to leave the deadness of guilt and fear and experience the life of joy and peace. We begin to come to life.

The Power of Belief

I am who I believe I am. You are who I believe you are. God is who I believe he is. That which is valuable is what I believe to be valuable. What is right is what I believe to be right.

We live life according to our beliefs. Our beliefs actually control our lives. Our beliefs cause us to be optimistic or pessimistic. They cause us to think well of ourselves or disrespect ourselves. They determine what we think to be right or wrong. They cause us to feel responsible for ourselves or to expect others to care for us. What we believe is powerful in the functioning of our lives.

We believe certain things about God and what he does. We believe certain things about ourselves and our ways of living. We believe certain things about people and the ways they are and the ways they will behave. All of these beliefs impact our daily living. They contribute to our lives or they detract from our lives. They build up our lives or they tear down our lives.

If our beliefs are inaccurate to reality, we are in deep trouble. We are living lives of fantasy. If they are erroneous, our living may be disastrous. That which we believe will give us full and satisfying lives may actually be robbing us of our lives.

What we believe may be the single most important aspect of our lives when measuring happiness and fullness.

Jesus encountered faulty beliefs from the very beginning of his ministry. They were probably the subject of the discussions between the twelve year old Jesus and the rabbis. Later, he was constantly disagreeing with the Pharisees, lawyers, and scribes. Their understanding of God and his will was at odds with his knowledge. Their beliefs about how to measure and treat people were radically different than his. He rejected the lifestyle they taught and promoted. He said that their beliefs were killing their lives.

Beliefs direct behavior

Jesus said that what a person says and does are reflections of what he believes:

"A good man from out of the good treasure of his heart expresses that which is good. An evil man out of the evil treasure expresses that which is evil. His mouth speaks out of the overflow of his heart." (Jesus in Luke 6.45)

In the ancient world, the heart was the seat of understanding and belief. The stomach or bowels were the seats of emotion. When Jesus said that what is in a person's heart expresses itself in his speech and behavior, he is talking about what that person believes. Our beliefs express themselves in our behavior.

We are being destroyed by deadly, erroneous beliefs

Jesus revealed and taught that our lives are missing the mark because our understandings and beliefs miss the mark.

Jesus answered, "Truly, I say to you, everyone who practices error[1] is a slave to error. A slave does not live in the house forever, but the son lives there forever. If then the son should set you free, you shall be truly free." (Jesus in John 8.34-36)

Jesus taught that our basic problem in living life is that we are enslaved by misunderstanding, misguided behavior, and destructive lifestyles. Our beliefs are destructively wrong, and we need to be set free from those beliefs.

The power of wrong beliefs can be disastrous. Our most basic beliefs are not simply intellectual. They have deadly consequences for our living and our relationship with God.

So Jesus said to those Judeans who believed in him, "If you live by my teachings, you are truly my

---

[1] The Greek word *hamartia* is almost always translated as "sin" in the New Testament by English translators. This is done in spite of the fact that it has many synonyms. The correct word to be used of the many synonyms is determined by the context in which the word is found. In this case, Jesus is talking about truth. The opposite of truth is error.

disciples. You shall know the truth, and the truth shall set you free." (Jesus in John 8.31-32)

Jesus was constantly speaking about the truth. He said that he was revealing the truth to the world, and that truth could change life. He spoke constantly of having a message[2] from God that gives life to those who believe it because it reveals the truth. (John 5.24-25)

Life comes from believing Jesus

English translators often confuse the biblical verses that make this point by saying that we are to believe "on" Jesus. We are actually to believe in Jesus and in his revelations and teachings. We cannot separate who he is from his revelations. He lived his message, and that message sets us free to be whom God wants us to be.

The New Testament writers constantly emphasized belief as the secret to life. Belief in Jesus and his teachings make it possible for us to have the life of God in us. Through believing we begin to think like God thinks and behave like God behaves. We begin to have the life of the heavens and of eternity. We become spiritual offspring of the Heavenly Father.

---

[2] **Message** is a better English translation of the Greek word *logos* than is "word." Word must be further defined to be understandable. Message points us immediately to the content of what Jesus did and said.

Those who did accept him, he gave to them the power to be offspring of God, to those who believe in his name.[3] (John 1.12)

Believing the wrong things robs us of the fullness of life

Jesus said that believing the wrong things is our actual condition. We have been lied to and deceived, and we have believed the lies. We believe the lies about God, about other people, about ourselves, and about how to live life. We are people who have been imprisoned by falseness and fantasy and our lives are being destroyed by the falseness. (See John 8.31forward)

Jesus referred to us as dead people. We are the walking, living dead. We are not alive to the degree God intends for us to be because we are trapped in beliefs that take the life out of us. We become satisfied with life that is far less than we are meant to have. Paul stated this fact in his letter to the Romans:

All have missed the mark and are less than the wonderfulness that God intends. (Romans 3.23)

Jesus came to set us free from that which is killing us, and to give us understandings that give us life. He revealed the truth about God, about us, and about living. And the truth is wonderfully life-giving.

------

[3] **In his name** is an idiom that means "according to his teachings".

We must only believe it to receive the life he has planned for us.

Jesus addressed numerous beliefs that are common to all persons. These beliefs destroy the fullness of life that everyone is pursuing. They are beliefs that are promoted by the "world".

God is legalistic and harsh in his punishments.

I am less important than other people.

I should treat people exactly as they deserve to be treated.

I should take care of number one however necessary.

My goals justify the means I use to reach them.

No one is really honest.

I should destroy my competitors.

I should be "one of the bunch" in values and behavior.

I allow my sex drive to have free expression.

Possessions determine my value in society.

Leadership positions give my life superior value.

Always repay hurts done to me by others.

Never forget a wrong done to me or a favor done for me.

Criticize mistakes in persons in order to bring about change in them.

Be in competition with everyone.

Tomorrow is filled with fears.

We must change our beliefs in order to have real life

The Greek word *metanoia* is universally translated into English as "repentance." This is not the most accurate meaning of the word. Repentance means to feel sorry for or guilty for past wrongs. *Metanoia* means to change our thinking or understanding, to change our minds. It is used in the New Testament to mean to change our beliefs.

God cannot set us free from missing the mark if we will not change our ways of thinking and believing. We are trapped in lies and deceptions and cannot escape them if we will not believe differently.

Believing in Jesus is the key to new life. Jesus revealed, taught, and demonstrated the truth. If we will believe in him and what he has shown us, we can become "new creations in Christ." We can experience his promise of overflowing life.

"I have come that you may have life and have it to the overflow." (Jesus in John 10.10)

Jesus answered her, "Everyone who drinks this water will thirst again, but whoever will drink the water which I will give him shall in no way thirst forever. The water which I will give him shall become a spring of water in him, surging up into the life of God." (John 4.13-14)

Beliefs are the key. Believing lies robs us of life. Believing Jesus gives us life. Jesus is *the way, the truth, and the life.*

What are these life-giving truths that Jesus revealed? We must find them, believe them, and have life.

"The lamp of the body is the eye. Therefore, if your eye is healthy, your whole body will be full of light. But if your eye is defective, your whole body will be full of darkness. Therefore, if the light that is in you is darkness, how great is the darkness!" (Jesus in Matthew 6.22-23)

The Jesus message about a happy, gifting God, his spirit of gifting joy, his love for us, and his ways of living a lifestyle of joy, shares truths to us that we would never have dreamed were true. When we hear this message, believe its truthfulness, and commit ourselves to be God's kind of persons, our spirits and lives begin to be born again. We believe and begin to receive.

Truths that Make Life Different

Jesus said that he was revealing the truth and that truth had the power to set us free from life- and spirit-killing lies. (John 8.31ff) He said that his message has the power to give life to dead people in the here and now. These are strange statements. They seem impossible.

If the message of Jesus has the power that he said that it does, what are the contents of this powerful message? What are these truths that can set us free? What did he teach that can change the spirit and lives of persons when they believe it?

Jesus' message about God

We have already reviewed his revolutionary understandings of God, his spirit, his personality, and his behavior. He painted a portrait of God that is completely different than that normally believed by everyone.

We seldom understand what a profound difference our beliefs about God make in our minds and lifestyle. If we believe him to be detached, critical, judging, and angry, the belief causes us to be acutely aware of our shortcomings and mistakes. It causes us to have guilt about who we are as persons. It causes us to fear what God will do to us in the future when he rewards us with what we deserve. Believing in a legalistic and judgmental God actually scares the life out of us. It prevents peace, joy, and love, from possessing us.

For most people, God is bad news. He is not helping them to have life now, he is waiting to judge them in the future. What a spirit killer! Having that belief hanging over our heads is a sure way to take the joy out of our lives.

For most people, the happenings of our lives are rewards from God, especially the bad things that happen to us. We are not as aware of the good in our lives as we are the bad. When the bad happens we blame God and ourselves. We are convinced that we are being punished for our shortcomings and sins. We live in fear that some other punishment is just around the corner. We become spiritually pessimistic.

Jesus showed us an entirely different God with an entirely different spirit and personality. He showed us a God of gift-giving joy. Jesus was not nearly so interested in judging people as he was in giving them life. He had compassion for persons trapped in lifestyles, situations, and understandings that were stealing life from them. God sent him to help us escape our enslavement to those beliefs and have life.

Jesus demonstrated God as our Father who loves us and wants to gift us with life, joy, and fullness. He did not show us a God of guilt and punishment. He said that we have been lied to about who God is and what he is doing with us. If we believe Jesus' message, we begin to think about the person and actions of God in wonderfully different ways.

Rather than concentrating on righteousness, sin, blame, guilt, and fear, we can begin to look for the gifts of joy that God is showering down on us daily. We can begin to enjoy the grace that he is giving to us. We can begin to enjoy the love that he is having for us. All of this creates peace and joy in us and in our daily living. We begin to become different people in our spirits and relationships. We begin to have happy hearts, and we share that joy with those who are in our lives.

Jesus' message about all of us

We normally believe that we should treasure good people and despise bad people. Jesus showed us how to treasure everyone. He did call a spade a spade, however. He called some people snakes because they were snakes. And yet, he let them be snakes. He knew that they were enslaved by lies about God and about him. They were blind, lost, and dead in spirit.

Jesus showed us that God is all about people. Jesus cared about nothing else in his world like he cared about people. He did not care about politics, social ills, or the movement of nations as much as he cared about people trapped in death dealing beliefs.

He said that God knows everything about us because he cares that much for us. We are his prized creations. Nothing else is as valuable to him as are we.

Jesus said that the heavens burst forth in singing and celebration when we begin to believe, receive his spirit, and behave as he wants. When a sheep is found or a prodigal returns, it is time to have a party. Nothing compares to the love of God for us.

God cares so much for us that he sent Jesus to help us become free and to help us have life. We are his treasure. We can rejoice and be happy that the Father values and cares for us so much. He showers us with gifts of joy every day. We just do not have eyes to see and ears to hear, until we begin to believe the message of Jesus.

Jesus' message about other people

We normally believe that we are at the mercy of the actions of other people, that we are dependent on how they treat us, both badly and well. We become reactionary to who they are and what they do to and for us.

Jesus changed this kind of believing and thinking. He taught that we behave toward other people in specific ways in spite of how they may relate to us. He said we have the total initiative. Our actions do not depend on theirs, our actions are inspired by a God of gift-giving grace.

The basic idea behind the biblical idea of forgiveness is that we release ourselves from the effects of what other people do to us. They may cause us to suffer, but they do not determine how we respond to that suffering. We respond with grace no matter what the other person is doing.

The second Great Commandment to *agape* our neighbors is a directive to treat them with gifts of blessing and joy as our consistent lifestyle. This approach is not controlled by what they do or do not do. We will be who we are and act as we behave irrespective of the actions of others. We will be people of gift-giving grace just like our Father. We are his offspring. We are like him.

When we begin to live the gift-giving lifestyle we begin to have a level of life that is wonderful. Making people happy makes us even more happy. Giving life away helps us to have life.

When we believe in being persons of grace and *agape*, we begin to become full of life.

New beliefs create new spirits

When we begin to believe in the revelations and teachings of Jesus we begin to think and understand differently. His teachings reflect a different kind of spirit than what we have always known. They reflect a spirit of gift-giving graciousness, joy, happiness, and peace.

Most of us are not normally possessed of this kind of spirit. We long to have a life like Paul described in Galatians 5.22, but living seems to prevent us from experiencing it.

Now that we know that the spirit of God is a spirit of grace and *agape*, we know that we can be possessed by that same spirit. We can become his spiritual offspring. We can have his spirit in us. But, not without belief.

If we do not believe in grace and *agape*, and if we do not believe that God is seeking to put that spirit in us, we will never experience that fullness of life.

Jesus said that we must stay close to him in order to experience the life of God in us.

"Live in me, and I in you. For the branch is not able to bear fruit from itself, it must be connected to the vine. Neither can you unless you live in me. I am the vine, you are the branches. He who lives in me, and I in him, will bear much fruit. Because separated from me, you cannot accomplish anything." (John 15.4-5)

When we hear the message of Jesus, understand its meaning for us, and embrace its truths for our own, we begin to experience the new life from God, life from above. It changes who we are and how we live. It opens the door for the spirit of God to come into us and express itself in our personalities and behavior. We become born from above.

We are his creation, fashioned through Christ Jesus for good lifestyles, which God determined long ago that we should live according to them. (Ephesians 2.10)

Do not be fashioned according to this world. Be remade by the renewing of your beliefs, and you will demonstrate the good and acceptable and whole will of God. (Romans 12.2)

Believing and Receiving

The Gospel books are filled with the revelations of Jesus about the truth. They inform us about God, about us, about other people, and about living life. The revelations of Jesus paint a picture for us that is different than what we have always believed about all of these subjects.

His revelations show us why life is not full to overflowing like we dream that it can be. We are trapped in understandings and beliefs that take the joy and life out of us. We need to be reborn from the inside out. We need to see God, us, and living in new ways. We need to believe in Jesus.

One of our biggest hurdles in experiencing new life is inadequate translations of the Greek New Testament. Translators have been reluctant to use words that reveal the joy of Jesus and his Father. They have seldom caught the vision of what kind of Spirit is seen in the pages they are translating. They have been trapped in mindsets that skew the message in favor of ancient, orthodox state religion.

We must find ways to break out of traditional understandings that hide the truths of Jesus. The task is not as difficult as it may seem. As we study the many teachings and demonstrations that the Gospel writers record, we can see the flow of spirit that is there. We can see the personality of Jesus shine through. We can be captured by his joy and peace.

But to have his gift to us, we must walk with him in our living, and submit our hearts and lives to the Father. We must humbly walk with God in the ways Jesus revealed. As we do, we begin to become persons with new lifestyles and new spirits. We begin to be reborn as persons.

As time goes by our attitudes and personalities will change to be like that of the Father and the Son. We must study his teachings and dwell on his understandings. We must allow his mind to become ours. To the degree that we can do this, we can receive the life that he came to give to us.

God wants us to have lives that overflow with joy and peace. He wants us to share that gift with everyone else in our lives. Life is to be had because Jesus came and shared it with us. But, we must believe to receive. We must learn the message and believe it. Therein is life.

Jesus answered her, "Everyone who drinks this water will thirst again, but whoever will drink the water which I will give him shall in no way thirst forever. The water which I will give him shall become a spring of water in him, surging up into eternal life." (John 4.13-14)

Book Two: The Details of the Jesus Message

Part One: Characteristics of the Jesus Message

A Message of Truth

Pilate said, "Then you are a king?"
Jesus answered, "You say that I am a king. **But this is why I was born, and this is why I came into the world: that I may witness to the truth.** *Everyone who loves the truth listens to my voice."*
Pilate said, "What is truth?" (John 18.37-38)

The message of Jesus is a message that reveals truth about God, people, and life. Jesus told Pilate in no uncertain terms that he came into the world to reveal the truth. That witnessing to the truth was the reason he was born and the reason he was in the world.

The Gospel of John follows this theme throughout its pages. Jesus is revealing the truth about God as he has never been revealed before. Jesus shows us the Father with awesome new insight. Jesus describes him and demonstrates his personality by means of his own personality, lifestyle, and teachings.

Humanity constantly misunderstands God

Jesus' mission of truth is necessary because God is not accurately known and understood by the world at large. In fact, he is radically misunderstood and mischaracterized. Jesus came to correct that situation.

Jesus was speaking to some of the most religious people on Earth when he said:

Jesus said, "If God were your father, you would have been gracious to me, because I came from God and am here. I have not come on my own, but he sent me with a message.

"Why do you not understand my message? Because you are unable to hear and accept my teachings. You are from a diabolic father, and the passions of your father you want to pursue. He was a killer from the beginning, and did not stand for truth, because truth is not in him.

"Whenever he speaks deceitfully, he speaks from himself, because he is a liar and the father of liars. Because I speak the truth, you do not believe me." (John 8.42-45)

The sad shape of the world is that it lives in the darkness of misunderstanding about God, people and life. But, the misunderstanding is not simply ignorance. It is life-destroying misunderstanding. Jesus states above that the lies people believe are diabolical and they kill the spirit and life in people. People pursue life with misunderstandings that kill their spirits, their joy, their relationships, and their peace. God sent his son to reveal the truth about all of these things, and that truth has powerful results in the lives of those who believe his message.

Jesus said to those Judeans who were believing in him, "If you live by my teachings, you are truly my disciples. You shall know the truth, and the truth shall set you free." (John 8.31-32)

The Jesus message is good news

The revelations and teachings of Jesus are marvelously good. They are called the Good News because they are wonderfully so. The truth he reveals is astoundingly life changing in the best of ways.

Jesus paints a picture of God by means of his teachings and his own demonstrations that has never been painted before by any religion. He not only testifies to what is true. He demonstrates it by means of his own spirit and behavior.

__The message became flesh and blood and lived among us__, and we recognized his glory, glory like that of an only child of a father, overflowing with grace and truth. (John 1.14)

Philip said to him, "Lord, show us the Father, and it will satisfy us."
Jesus said to him, "Have I been with you such a long time, Philip, and you still do not understand me? __He who has seen me has seen the Father.__ How can you still say, 'Show us the Father?'" (John 14.8-9)

This last statement by Jesus is a statement of revelation. If one wants to know how the Father behaves and what kind of spirit and attitudes he has, all he has to do is observe Jesus. Jesus was the living demonstration. He was the living message from God.

Jesus is the standard of God

Understandings of God in any religion or philosophy that are different from those shown and taught by Jesus are inaccurate or untrue. Those that are consistent with his message and revelations are true. Jesus is the touchstone and the cornerstone. He is the plumb line by which all understandings of God and his ways must be judged and measured. One cannot truly know who God is and what he is doing without the message of Jesus. His revelations are true, accurate, and real.

There is only one God and one mediator between God and men, himself man, Christ Jesus. (1Timothy 2.5)

Faith is believing in Jesus and his message

Many seers and prophets have come into the world with messages about the person of God and his will for mankind. Each has a unique understanding of the truth. But they disagree. Whom shall we believe is accurate and true?

Followers of Jesus believe in him and his revelations. They trust him to be true to reality. He is not a purveyor of fantasy and imagination. He shows us the Father as he really is.

If the message of Jesus is the only completely accurate one on Earth, his followers must protect, preserve, and publish it worldwide. How will others know its powerful truths unless they are informed?

Jesus commissioned his followers to take his message and teachings to everyone as one of his last acts on Earth.

"Therefore, go and make students of all peoples, immersing them in the name of the Father and the Son and the Holy Spirit, teaching them to practice all that I instructed you; and lo, I am with you always, even to the end of the age." (Jesus in Matthew 28.19-20)

What is the content of this powerful message? What are the important facts that Jesus revealed? What information is so affective that it can change the hearts and lives of any person who believes? These are the most important questions facing us in this study.

We must discover the truths that Jesus came to reveal to us. We must discover why they are called "good" news. We must learn how to understand this good news and be able to communicate it to other people.

Jesus is the Message

*God, having in times past spoken to our ancestors through the prophets, in various fragments and by various means, has in these last days spoken to us in his Son, whom he appointed the receiver of all things, through whom also he made the age; **who being the reflection of his glory, and the very image of his character,** and under girding all these things with his powerful message, when he had cleansed us from 'missing the mark', sat down on the right hand of the Majesty on high. Having become so much better than other messengers, so that he has received a name more excellent than they.* (Hebrews 1.1-4)

The message of God has come to us through the person of his son Jesus. Jesus taught and demonstrated his message, because his message is about life, living, and relationships. The message is about personality and the individual spirits in persons. Jesus taught about these things and demonstrated them in the living of his life. He showed us God and his ways as well as he told us about them. He was the personification of God's message to humanity.

All religions paint pictures of God and his ways with humans. They attempt to satisfy the curiosity of mankind about the invisible things of the spirit world. Each religion has its answers to basic spiritual questions.

People in Jesus' life had the same curiosity. The rich, young ruler asked about the life of God which Jesus had been teaching,

A certain ruler asked him, saying, "Good teacher, what can I do to receive life of the heavens?[4]" (Luke 18.18)

The young man had life, but for him it was an incomplete life. He knew there was more and he had probably heard Jesus talking about his abundant, overflowing life. Jesus had spoken of God's life, life of the heavens, life that never ends. This man who had everything the world has to offer knew that what he had was not enough.

Philip asked Jesus to show him who God really is in John 14.8-9. In this context, Jesus is making a statement about the content of his teachings and revelations. Jesus was saying that God is like him in attitude, values, spirit, personality, and behavior. In short, God acts like Jesus acts and has his personality. If this is true, it causes multitudes of problems for all religions. No religion has ever portrayed God to be like Jesus in personality and behavior.

Jesus proclaimed his exclusivity of portrayal and relationship in a much misunderstood statement

---

[4] The Greek phrase "life of the eons of the eons" is what is being translated here. It is usually translated using one of two English words: eternal or everlasting. However, the emphasis does not appear to be on the length of life as much as the kind of life. It is life like that of God. It is life like that lived in the heavens, heavenly life.

about knowing the Father. The seeming exclusivity of the statement is not directed at indicting persons who do not know Jesus. It is a statement that supports the truth of his revelations about the Father. To know God as he truly is, one must learn from Jesus. All other understandings and revelations are inadequate.

Jesus said to him, "I am the way, and the truth, and the life. No one comes to [know] the Father, if not through me. If you have known me, you have known my Father also. From now on you know him, and have seen him." (John 14.6-7)

Beliefs: Philosophical or Behavioral?

Religious beliefs run the gamut from philosophical to behavioral. Some are merely intellectual, others impact daily living. The message of Jesus is powerfully behavioral. His teachings are about life and it's living.

True, he revealed intellectual understandings of God and life, but those understandings were ones that make a difference in daily life.

Jesus revealed the personality of God and his ways of acting. In so doing, he changes our perceptions of our own lives and how we should live them.

Jesus revealed the characteristics of the human condition and helps us understand the influences they have on our spirits and behavior. When we believe what he taught, our perceptions of life, and our relationships with God and other people can change drastically.

Jesus revealed a different approach to lifestyle that leads to a fullness of living that changes whom we are as persons. It speaks to our daily behavior in awesome and wonderful ways. It changes us as persons. Not just intellectually or philosophically, but behaviorally. His message to us creates a new kind of person in all areas of our living.

It is no wonder that John was much more interested in the spirits of persons than he was in their religious proclamations. In his first letter he cautioned the churches to pay attention to the spirit and lifestyle of persons more than to their religious positions.

Gracious ones, do not believe every spirit, but test the spirits to see if they are of God. Because many pseudo-prophets have voyaged out into the world. (1 John 4.1)

John spends the rest of chapter four describing the gracious *agape* spirit and behavior that is characteristic of God and those who believe in him. He is very practical in his presentation of what is important to God. He speaks most powerfully about lifestyle and personal relationships.

Gracious ones, we should be gracious to one another because graciousness is of God. Anyone who is gracious has been fathered by God and understands God. One who is not a person of grace has not understood God, because God is gracious. (1 John 4.7-8)

The revelation of grace and graciousness is all about personal spirit and behavior. Grace has little meaning when not expressed in action. When it is expressed, it is a distinct kind of behavior that blesses everyone involved. Believing in a God of grace and a lifestyle of gracious living transforms spirit and lifestyle. It is intellectual, but it is intellectual belief about daily behavior.

If a brother or sister be naked and in lack of daily food, and one of you says to them, "Go in peace, be you warmed and filled," and yet you do not give them the things needed by the body, what good did it do? Even so, belief, if it is not expressed in behavior, is dead in itself.

"Yes," a man will say, "you have belief, and I have actions. Show me your belief apart from your behavior, and I will show you my beliefs by my lifestyle." (James 2:15-18)

The Message is Often Stifled

John said:

The light shines in the darkness, and the darkness cannot snuff it out. (John 1.5)

The darkness could not snuff out the mission, ministry, and message of Jesus in spite of its many attempts. But forces at work in the world have seriously stifled the message throughout its history. The light has not been destroyed, but it has been sidetracked and misrepresented often. The two most detracting forces have been institutional religion and misleading language.

The Spirit was institutionalized

Beginning with Constantine the Great in the early AD 300s, the Christian message was forced into the mold of a state religion. That which was a movement of the Spirit of God that transformed the spirits of individuals was redesigned to fulfill the needs of a political religion. The free flow of an invisible spirit was transformed into a religion into which every citizen could be inducted whether or not he or she actually believed the transforming revelations of Jesus.

The Roman emperors needed a religious glue to hold their fragile empire together. They needed a common faith for all of their people in order to overcome the many racial and religious fractures in the widespread empire.

The need for a personal spiritual experience was pushed aside in favor of initiation rites that could be applied to all citizens without hesitation. The Empire needed for everyone to be a member of its state religion. Any requirement that hampered that membership could not be perpetuated. Membership became institutional rather than spiritual.

The message of Jesus about being possessed of a new spirit that in turn molded the personality and lifestyle of a person after that of the Heavenly Father, turned to new and less esoteric emphases. All citizens were expected to become a part of the state church by means of a baptismal rite. That rite itself was understood to be magical in its ability to free the soul from past sin and set it on a course for heaven.

The original emphasis on having new life now within each believer transitioned into being concerned about getting into heaven at the end of life. The state church claimed the power to determine who could enter heaven and who could not. This gave the institution awesome power over the citizens of the realm. The threat of excommunication from the church was a threat of exclusion from heaven itself.

What a powerful political tool in the hands of the state. The original message of freedom and overflowing personal life had been stifled in favor of political ends useful to emperors and empires.

The Message was misunderstood

The second stifling phenomenon was the translation of the written message into secondary languages. The original Greek manuscripts were translated into numerous languages in the Eastern world, and into Latin in the Western world. By AD 500, all of these languages were attempting to communicate the original message of Jesus and his mission.

It is no wonder that there were disagreements among Christians worldwide. The many language versions of the life and message of Jesus contained differing understandings of them.

Translations are never automatic. Words in one language may have several possibilities for translation in another. Translators must choose words that they understand to be the most consistent with the originals. Therein lie huge problems for the message of Jesus. If translators are not on the same wavelength as Jesus and his disciples, their translations do not accurately communicate the story.

Original New Testament writings were penned by persons who had personal knowledge of Jesus, or they knew persons who did (as in Luke, who traveled with Paul). They knew much more than they committed to writing. That additional knowledge helped them to accurately understand what had been written. They were not limited to the New Testament texts for understandings. They knew many more teachings and actions. John made this point when he said:

This is the disciple who testifies about these things and who wrote these things, and we know that his testimony is true. There are many other things that Jesus did, that if were written one by one, not even the world itself could contain the books. (John 21.24-25)

First century Christians knew many of these other things that Jesus did and it assisted them in understanding the meaning of the biblical writings. As the years went by, that other material began to disappear. At first, each generation of church leaders claimed special knowledge from those who had gone before. The "apostolic tradition" was born, and claimed to have the exclusive knowledge needed to accurately interpret what the written message meant. Apostolic succession became a political lever used to back up claims when there were disagreements with those who could not claim such connection.

However, the evidence of disagreements in understanding and application of Jesus' mission and message began earlier during the life of Paul. He disagreed with Peter at Antioch,

When Peter came to Antioch, I challenged him personally because he was at fault. (Galatians 2.11)

Paul mentioned to Timothy that he had strong disagreements with the churches in Asia Minor,

You know this, that all who are in Asia have turned away from me, including Phygelus and Hermogenes. (2 Timothy 1.15)

Paul cautioned the Corinthians to beware of those who proclaim different understandings of Jesus, the Spirit, and the message.

When one comes who proclaims a different Jesus, whom we have not proclaimed, or when you observe a different spirit, which you have not already received, or a different Good News, which you have not already accepted, you are too patient. (2 Corinthians 11.4)

Obviously, there was more than one apostolic tradition in the New Testament world. Differing lines of understanding and application were at work thirty years after the death of Jesus. This may be the reason that John penned his gospel near the end of the century. He wanted to reestablish the main message of Jesus and what it means to mankind.

John focused on the revelations of Jesus and their ability to move persons from death into life. John's gospel is all about the heavenly spirit coming down and inhabiting the bodies of believers. This presence of the Sprit of God in a life transformed that life into a life like that of the Father and the Son. His emphasis is on what God is doing with lives in the here and now.

"I did not recognize him, but he who sent me to immerse in water said to me, 'He upon whom you see the Spirit descending and remaining upon him, this is the one who immerses in the Spirit of God.'" (John the Baptist in John 1.33)

Paul wrote extensively about the presence of the Spirit in persons, and the creation of new spirits and lives in them because of that presence. He spoke of persons becoming new creations in Christ.

Both John and Paul evidently fought the battles to clarify who Jesus was and what he was about. They had difficulty breaking through mindsets that were fashioned by traditional religion, both Jewish and pagan. Their emphasis on personal transformation was a radical new understanding of what God is doing in Jesus. Jesus was not establishing a new religion. He was creating new persons who would make up a new spiritual kingdom on Earth.

The New Testament is filled with metaphors and parables that are understood differently by many believers. The disagreements about which words to understand literally and which to understand symbolically continue to this day. Christians strongly disagree with each other about the intended meaning of many verses.

These disagreements influence how the New Testament is translated into various languages. Translators obviously convey meanings that they understand. They select words that carry the meanings important to themselves. In some cases, they refuse to translate words that appear to disagree with their understandings or practices.

Baptidzo was not translated into English because it means to immerse and the church of the translators did not practice immersion. They chose to Anglicize the word to be "baptize" rather than to translate it.

Diaconos was not translated because it means a servant and in churches it has come to mean an office in the congregation. It was Anglicized to be "deacon."

There are many other words in the original Greek texts that have been skewed in translation to support a particular viewpoint or understanding. In so doing, the original message is stifled for the reader. A major task of the Bible student is to study enough and in depth enough to ferret out original meanings of biblical words and concepts. It is a daunting task.

We are including our own translation of the biblical texts to try and recapture some of those original meanings. We want the Bible to speak its message to us regardless of its disagreements with popular church understandings. God never intended for the Scripture to be a tool to be manipulated by the church for its own ends, no matter how noble they may seem.

The New Testament is about the message of God to us through his Son. We must let the message be what it is and refashion our understandings and applications as dictated by the Word. Otherwise, the message may be stifled by well meaning people.

New Testament Words
That Can Skew the Idea of Message

The oldest manuscripts that we have of the New Testament books are written in the Greek language. English translators have translated these manuscripts into English so that we may read them in our own language. The translators, obviously, do their very best to convey the original meanings of words and ideas by means of their translations.

However, conveying ideas from one language to another is not always simple and easy, and is never automatic. Words in one language may not have equivalent words in another language. This reality often causes ambiguity in the understanding of original intentions. When it does, some of the nuances of the original writings are lost in translation. This has happened with English translations of the New Testament in reference to the ideas of messenger and message.

Translators of any document translate from their understanding of what the content is about. Words in one language have numerous synonyms in another language that convey differing shades of meaning. Translators must choose the one from among these synonyms that they think best expresses the original intention of the writer. Their choices may have powerful consequences for the way the original message is understood by those reading their translations.

The Christian New Testament is filled with word options from which English translators must choose. One example is "sin." The word translated as "sin" is usually the Greek word, *hamartia*, which can be translated numerous ways depending on the context in which it is used. Translators universally choose to translate it as "sin" on every occasion. This results in some obscurity for the original message of the New Testament. The word means to be wrong, off target, in error, misunderstanding, and several other ideas. Translating it as "sin" every time it appears causes shades of meaning to be lost.

Our immediate concern is the translation of words and phrases related to the idea of message and messenger. The idea is very important to the mission of Jesus. If the concept of message gets lost in translation, we are handicapped in understanding what he was about at the core of his mission. We will look at some of the words in question.

Jesus told Pilate that the reason he was born was to reveal the truth to the world. (John 18.37-38) If the message of Jesus is skewed in some way, the truth that he came to communicate to the world is skewed also. At all costs we must strive to keep his revelations and teachings accurate.

Following are a few of the key words referring to message that have lost some of their meaning when English translators have brought the biblical text into English.

Angels

The Greek word *angelos* is transliterated into English as "angel". Note that this is not a translation. The Greek word has not actually been translated. It has simply been brought into English phonetically. The Greek has simply been Anglicized. It may be an acceptable rendering, but it loses the concept of an angel as a messenger. The word means to be a messenger. As a result of not translating the word, angels are simply thought of as spiritual beings with very little understanding of the messenger aspect of their being.

When Jesus said, *And he saith unto him, Verily, verily, I say unto you, Hereafter ye shall see heaven open, and the angels of God ascending and descending upon the Son of man.* (John 1.51 KJV), the idea of those angels being messengers from the Father drops out of the translation.

Verse 51 correlates with the sayings of Jesus later when he says to the Father, *the communications that you gave to me I have given to them; and they received them and truly understood that I came forth from you, and they believed that you sent me with a message.* (John 17.8)

Sometimes the failure to translate properly obscures the meaning of verses in the New Testament. Such is the case with Hebrews 1.4. *Having become so much better than other messengers, so that he has received a name more excellent than they.* Transliterating *angelos* as angels in this verse obscures its meaning that Jesus was far superior to all other messengers of God, so much so, that he received the name of "Son."

Of course, there are times when *angelos* simply means angels. Translators have the difficult task of deciding which use is intended in a given context.

Word

The Greek word *logos* is almost exclusively translated as "word" by English translators. This habit has been followed even though translators know that *logos* can also be translated as "speech," "message," "communication" and other synonyms that convey a similar meaning. In fact, translating *logos* as "word" is often a very poor translation. Good English would require that it at least be translated in the plural, "words", to convey its original intent.

"Message" is by far the more accurate translation of the ideas behind the Greek word *logos* in most instances in the New Testament. Saying that Jesus is the message of God to us communicates better than saying that he is the word of God to us. It resonates with the same ideas in Hebrews 1.1-2,

God, after he spoke long ago to the fathers through the prophets in many fragments and in many ways, in these last days has spoken to us in his Son, whom he appointed recipient of all things, through whom also he made the age.

The original texts emphasize that Jesus was a messenger with a message, but English translations often fail to convey those ideas because of the English words chosen and used by translators. An insistence that a Greek word like *logos* be translated in exactly the same way every time it appears is an artificial insistence. Doing so obscures the original message of the Bible. We will reflect various options in our translations of Bible passages.

Sent with a Message

An apostle is accurately understood to be one sent with a message. The verbal form of the Greek word, *apostello*, carries the same idea of sending one with a message.

The Greek New Testament uses two words that are usually translated as "sent" in English, *pempo* and *apostello*. *Pempo* means to be sent and is accurately translated as such in English translations. However, *apostello* is usually translated as sent also when it actually has far more meaning that is missed by that translation.

A more accurate translation of *apostello* is to be "sent with a message." A single English word will not contain all that is meant by the original. As a result, much of the meaning in some verses is missed. For example, the idea of Jesus being a messenger sent with a message disappears in verses like John 17.18, *As thou hast sent me into the world, even so have I also sent them into the world.* (KJV)

A more accurate translation would be, *"As you sent me into the world with your message, I have also sent them into the world with your message."* This more accurate translation adds richness to what Jesus is saying. He is not just sending his disciples into the world, he is sending them to share a message from God.

Jesus uses *apostello* often, but it is not apparent in most English translations. Better translations would convey the more subtle meanings of the Greek word.

The Good Message

The Greek word *euangelion* is usually translated as "gospel" in English translations. This practice obscures the original meaning by using an old English word that means "good news." When the ambiguous word "gospel" is used, it leaves room for all kinds of definitions to be applied to it. And theologians, preachers, and teachers become very creative in their definitions.

Notice that the stem word in *euangelion* is angel. Just as angel is about being a messenger, so this word is about a message. The *eu* added to the front of angel means "good." The resultant meaning is "good message." "Good news" is an OK translation, but once again the idea of a message from God drops out of the translation.

Further on the same subject, the verbal form, *euangelidzo*, is usually transliterated as "evangelize." Note that this is a transliteration rather than a translation. A more accurate translation would be "to tell the good message" or "share the good message." Too often, Christians understand evangelism to mean for one to be a soul-winner rather than a simple teller of the good message of Jesus.

The concept of a message from God communicated to the world by Jesus, and carried forth by his followers is central to the New Testament. Additionally, the New Testament shares the story of the effects of that message on those who heard it and believed it. The message contains an awesome power. It has the power to change the spirits, hearts, and lives of those who hear, accept and believe it.

God has not given us a spirit of timidity, but of power and graciousness and self-control. So, do not be ashamed of the message of our Lord or of me his prisoner. But join with me in suffering for the good message that demonstrates the power of God,

who has saved us and called us with a holy calling, not because of our works, but because of his own purpose and grace that was given to us in Christ Jesus from eternal times, and now has been revealed by the revelation of our Savior Christ Jesus, who nullified death and brought life and the imperishable to light through the good message, for which I was appointed a proclaimer and a messenger and a teacher. (2 Timothy 1.7-11)

A Message about Personal Spirits

Another one of the secrets hidden in the words of the New Testament concerns the spirits of persons. It speaks often of the kinds of spirits that inhabit persons. There are persons with unclean spirits, demonic spirits, legalistic spirits, unforgiving spirits, selfish spirits, and numerous other spirits that express themselves in personality and behavior.

The hidden aspect of these concepts is that the way in which the word spirit is used is very similar to our modern word "personality". Spirits express themselves in behavior, attitudes, and values. We normally label this area of thinking as personality rather than spirit, although we do speak of the spirits of persons on occasion. The subject becomes more clear for us when we use the word personality when the word spirit is applied to persons.

Paul demonstrated this truth when he described the expressions of the Spirit of God in the lives of persons:

The fruit [expression] of the Spirit is graciousness[5], joy, peace, patience, kindness, goodness, dependability, gentleness, self-control. No law can produce these characteristics. (Galatians 5.22-23)

---

[5] See below for a discussion about translating *agape* as graciousness rather than love.

The words he uses here are words that define personality and behavior. When the Spirit of God is in a life, that life takes on a new personality that is identifiable. Paul lists very observable personality traits that are characteristics of God's Spirit. They are characteristics of the heavenly. They demonstrate the life of the heavens in a person.

If we use the same words for God's Spirit as we do for our own and understand that the meaning behind the words is that of personality as well as spirit, we make a startling discovery. The Spirit of God is also the personality of God.

The words used by Paul above are descriptions of the personality of God. They are descriptions of his Spirit. We can say then, that when the Spirit of God is in us, we begin to have his personality. We can also say that when his personality is in us, we have eternal life, life of the heavens. We are becoming like the Father. We have his life in us. His personality gives us new life. It creates a new person and personality in our bodies. We become new creations through the message, demonstrations, and revelations of Jesus.

That is awesome! God puts his personality in us and makes us his spiritual offspring, or as the New Testament says it, "children of God". Jesus gave us the ability to become "sons of God". We have been born from above. His Spirit and personality have come down into us and given us life.

"Truly, I say to you, he who hears my message, and believes that [God] sent me, has life of the heavens, and has no need of condemnation, but has

passed out of death into life." (John 5.24)

We would never have known about the Spirit and personality of God if they had not been revealed to us by Jesus as part of his message. Nor would we have known that he wants to put his spiritual personality in us.

John the Baptist identified Jesus as one who came to immerse us in the Spirit and personality of God.

John bore witness saying, "I have seen the Spirit coming down like a dove out of heaven, and it dwelled in him. I did not know him, but the one who sent me to immerse in water, he said to me, 'Upon the one whom you see the Spirit descending and dwelling in him, it is he who immerses in the Spirit of God.'" (John 1.32-33)

James would write later:

By his own will he brought us forth by means of the message of truth, so that we might be a kind of first editions of his creations. (James 1.18)

This new creation is a kingdom of people who have the personality of God in themselves. Because they believe the message of Jesus, they become infused with God's presence and personality. They take on the glory that God has always wanted us to have. We are no longer "short of the glory." We are becoming like the Father and the Son.

A Message with Power

John said:

These things are written, so that you might believe that Jesus is the Anointed One, the Son of God; and by believing you might have life through his message. (John 20.31)

Paul said:

...but is now revealed through the demonstration of our Savior Jesus Christ, who has thwarted death. He has enlightened us about life and immortality through the Good News. (2 Timothy 1:10)

...how that our good message did not come to you in words only, but also in power, and in the Spirit of God, and in much assurance; even as you know what kind of men we showed ourselves to you for your sake. (1 Thessalonians 1.5)

My speech and my preaching was not with enticing words of man's wisdom, but in demonstration of the Spirit and of power: (1 Corinthians 2.4 KJV)

And Jesus said:

"It is the spirit that gives life. The flesh profits nothing. The words that I speak to you, they are spirit, and they are life." (John 6:63)

The message of Jesus has the awesome power to change people. When heard and believed, the message changes the attitudes, personalities, and lifestyles of persons. It did this in New Testament times and it still does the same in today's world. People meet and walk with the Father of Jesus Christ and they change in profound ways.

The difference that the message makes in people is observable. They become possessed of a different spirit and attitude than before. Their behavior changes in specific ways. The Book of Acts records this phenomenon as it happened to the Gentiles in Antioch of Syria.

"As I was speaking, the Spirit of God fell upon them just as it did upon us at the beginning. And I remembered the words of the Lord, how he used to say, 'John immersed us in water, but you will be immersed in the Spirit of God.' Therefore, if God also gave to them the same gift as he gave to us, after believing in the Lord Jesus Christ, who was I that I could stand in God's way?" (Peter in Acts 11.15-17)

The Spirit is expressed through personality

Peter and his friends saw something happen to those new believers in Antioch. They saw them become changed in spirit, attitude, and behavior. Paul would identify these changes in people later when he wrote to the Galatian Christians:

The fruit [expressions] of the Spirit is graciousness, joy, peace, patience, kindness, goodness, dependability, gentleness, self-control. No law can produce these characteristics. (Galatians 5.22-23)

The fruit of the Spirit can also be understood to mean the expressions of the Spirit. The presence could only be detected as it was observed by changes in the personality of the believer. The characteristics listed by Paul above are characteristics of a person's personality. When we receive the Spirit of God, we receive his personality. We begin to be like him. We begin to be immersed in his Spirit and in his personality.

When the message was shared, the Spirit fell upon persons. They became immersed in the Spirit of God. They became "born from above." The fruit or expression of this immersion could be observed. They began to behave like Paul described. The message that was shared had a power to transform hearts and lives. And the transformation was beautiful to behold. Ordinary people became glorious people with new and different personalities.

This ability to transform lives is the "power" of the Good News spoken of in the New Testament. The message of Jesus was not just an intellectual exercise in mental belief. It issued forth in powerful life-changing experiences.

Legalistic persons became gracious.
Unhappy persons became joyous.
Cantankerous persons became peaceful.
Aggressive persons became patient.
Uncaring persons became kind.
Bad persons became good.
Undependable persons became faithful.
Harsh persons became gentle.
Overly passionate persons became more in control of their lives. (Galatians 5.22-23)

This picture is one of an unbelievably attractive kind of people. They were living demonstrations of the power of the message of Jesus and the Spirit that attends it. With results like this, it is no wonder that it was called the "Good" News.

A Message Supported by Miracles

There was a Pharisee named Nicodemus, a leader of the Judeans, who came to Jesus in the night, and said to him, "Rabbi, we know that you are a teacher who has come from God, because no one is able to do the signs which you do unless God is with him." (John 3.1-2)

The peoples of the world have always been fascinated by miracles. They like to believe that there are persons who can do things that are unexplainable. Religion has often been validated by events that defy natural explanation. They are supernatural happenings, filled with magic.

Jesus Christ was one of those religious leaders who did miraculous things. He healed the sick, calmed winds, restored sight, created wine and other foods, and walked on water. His life was attended by miraculous happenings. He said that he did these miraculous things so that people would believe in him. They were validations of his relationship to God and his revelations from God.

Unlike magicians, Jesus did not do miracles for his own prosperity. He was not seeking social position or wealth. In fact, he said that he had come to give his life for others. His magic was not for the same purposes as those of other magicians. It was a simple method of proving that he was actually speaking for the Living God. It was proof of his credentials. It was a means of convincing people that the rest of his mission was initiated by God and approved by God. This miraculous part of his ministry was described as "power" by his disciples. Their message and mission was characterized by that same "power."

even Jesus of Nazareth, how God anointed him with the Holy Spirit and with power: who went about doing good things, and healing all who were oppressed by the devil; because God was with him. (Acts 10:38)

And Stephen, full of faith and power, did great wonders and miracles among the people. (Acts 6:8 KJV)

My speech and my preaching were not in persuasive words of wisdom, but in demonstration of the Spirit and of power: that your faith should not stand on the wisdom of men, but on the power of God. (Paul in 1 Corinthians 2:4-5)

The most life-changing part of the mission of Jesus was the miraculous power of his message. This magical phenomenon has been greatly neglected by the church because it is so elusive and unpredictable. The miraculous message of Jesus has the power to this day to change the life of an individual. It is miraculous because it causes life changes in uncontrollable ways. People change when they accept and believe in Jesus and his message.

Jesus spoke of this himself,

Truly, I say to you, he who hears my message, and believes in him who sent me, has eternal life, and comes not into condemnation, but has moved out of death into life. (John 5:24)

In ordinary language Jesus is saying that persons who hear his message, believe that it is from God and accept it, can have a life-changing experience. They are awakened to a new kind of life, and it is eternal, it is God's kind of life.

The uniqueness of this experience is in the kind of life that is created in these persons who believe. The changes wrought in them are not mysterious abilities to do the miraculous themselves. The changes are in the creation of a marvelous spirit and lifestyle. They become people of grace. They become wonderful examples of living life in ways that are appreciated by the people whom they touch.

The Message of Jesus has Awesome Power

"Make them godly by means of the truth; your message is truth." (Jesus to God, John 17.17)

In keeping with his will, he birthed us again by the message of truth, so that we would be a kind of first edition among his creations. (James 1.18)

Therefore, putting aside all filthiness and all that remains of wickedness, humbly receive the message that has been implanted in you, that has the power to save your souls. (James 1.21)

"You are already clean because of the message I have spoken to you." (Jesus in John 15.3)

You have been reborn, not from seed that is perishable but imperishable, that is, through the living and enduring message of God. (1 Peter 1.23)

The message of Jesus is not simply wise information for living well in this life. It is not simply instructions for good morality. It is not the promotion of a lifestyle that produces health and wealth.

The message of Jesus is a message from God that has wonderful life-changing effects in the hearts and lives of individuals. When understood and believed, the message causes a rebirth of spirit within persons. This new spirit in turn expresses itself in a different lifestyle than before. Attitudes, values, goals, and understandings change. The message is that revolutionary, and it possesses an almost mystical power to change people and their lives. It gives to them a fullness of life that was not being experienced before.

Therefore, if any man is in Christ, he is a new creature. The old things have passed away. Behold, they have become new. (2 Corinthians 5:17)

...like newborn infants, naturally long for the wholesome milk of the message, so that by it you may grow into salvation, (1 Peter 2.2)

Belief Without Behavior is Meaningless

Can a person believe in Jesus but not practice the lifestyle which he taught? James did not think so, as stated in the verses above. Nor did John think so as is indicated in his statement,

By this we know that we know him, if we practice his instructions. He who says, "I know him", and does not practice his teachings, is a liar, and the truth is not in him. (1 John 2.3-4)

We often forget that Jesus behaved like and was considered to be a teacher by those around him. He was called Rabbi, the Hebrew word for teacher. He was also referred to as Master, which is the old English word for teacher. He traveled around the country with his disciples, a word which identifies them as students of a teacher.

Jesus was very adamant about the need for his students to practice what he was teaching them.

Therefore, Jesus said to those Jews who had believed him, "If you live out my message, then you are truly my disciples [students]." (John 8.31)

In addition, he commissioned his students to go and make students of everyone else.

"Therefore, go and make students of all peoples, immersing them in the name of the Father and the Son and the Holy Spirit, teaching them to practice all that I instructed you; and lo, I am with you always, even to the end of the age." (Matthew 28.19-20)

"If you keep my instructions, you shall live according to my graciousness; even as I have kept my Father's instructions, and live according to his graciousness." (John 15.10)

"He who has my instructions, and practices them, it is he who makes me happy: and he who makes me happy shall be made happy by my Father, and I will be gracious to him, and will reveal myself to him." (Jesus in John 14.21)

Part Two: Foundations of the Jesus Message

The message of Jesus rests on two basic foundational concepts. They are the keys to understanding the many details of his teachings and revelations. They are always hovering in the background of everything that takes place in the New Testament. Without an understanding of them, the message revealed by Jesus and proclaimed by his apostles is very difficult to comprehend.

The first concept is that of grace. Grace is too often misunderstood to be a complicated theological and philosophical doctrine very difficult to grasp by the uninitiated. Quite the opposite is true. Grace is a simple concept, but a profound one. The concept of grace runs through all of the teachings and revelations of Jesus about God and about the eternal lifestyle.

The second concept is that involving the Greek words *agape* and *agapao*. The words are central to the message. They appear everywhere in New Testament scripture. They are usually translated as "love" in English translations of the New Testament but actually have far more profound meaning than that single idea. Misunderstanding these words means to miss the central idea of the Jesus Message.

The following chapters explore the background, meaning, and applications of these words and concepts. They are foundational to all other insight into the unique revelations of Jesus. We would never have known about grace and *agape* had Jesus not come and revealed them to us by means of his own life and his teachings. They actually turn the religious world upside down.

Foundations on
Which the Jesus Message Rests

*"Teacher, which is the greatest commandment
in the law?" He said to him, "You shall be gracious
to the Lord you God with all your heart, and with all
your soul, and with all your mind. This is the great
and first commandment. A second like it is this, you
shall be gracious to your neighbor as yourself. On
these two commandments the whole law hangs, and
the prophets."* (Matt. 22:36-40)

*Know this, you shall not commit adultery, you
shall not murder, you shall not steal, you shall not
covet, and if there is any other commandment, it is
captured in this phrase, specifically, you shall be
gracious to your neighbor just as you are to yourself.*
(Romans 13.9)

The many lifestyle teachings of Jesus are all
constructed on the foundation of the two Great
Commandments. They define the kind of relationship
that should exist between us and God and us and other
people.

The depth of the meaning of these two
commandments has often been obscured by the way in
which they are normally translated into English. They
universally contain the word "love" as the translation
of *agape*. Following our discussion above about a
more accurate translation it is obvious that most of the

117

meaning of the commandments is lost by this translation. The emphasis on grace in *agape* is lost in translation.

Gifting God with our behavior

When we understand that Jesus was commanding us to be gifting toward the Father, it adds a wonderful dimension to the command. The basic idea in the word grace is good gift or good gifting. *Agape* carries the same core idea. To *agape* God is to give him good gifts from a full heart.

Our natural propensity is to think of God as one whom we are constantly beseeching to give us gifts. Our petitions to him are usually along that line of thinking and praying. Jesus said that God is doing that already because he is a gifting God who delights in giving good gifts to his children.

"Then, if you, being imperfect, know how to give good gifts to your children, how much more does your Father who is in heaven give good things to those who ask him?" (Matthew 7.11)

"Therefore, do not be anxious, saying, 'Where will we get food?' or, 'Where will we get drink?' or, 'Where will we get clothing?' The Gentiles pursue all of these things; but your heavenly Father already knows that you need all of these things." (Matthew 6.31-32)

The idea that we should be constantly giving good gifts to the Father is a new way of relating to him. He is constantly blessing us with good gifts and he is delighted when we return the favor. Just as we are pleased when someone gives us gifts, so is he pleased when we do the same for him.

The gifting idea conjures up images of persons who delight in gifting the Father. It speaks to the kind of hearts they have. They are full of love and gratitude and overflow with gifts to their Father who is outgiving them. Paul was on this same wavelength when he said:

Therefore, I appeal to you, brothers and sisters, because of the kindnesses of God, to present your bodies as living offerings; holy, pleasing to God, which is your logical way to serve him. (Romans 12.1)

The gifts the Father desires from his children are the gifts of the behavior that Jesus taught. When we forgive, go second miles, be patient, return good for bad, pray for our persecutors and generally live lives of gracious gifting to those around us, we are giving good gifts to our Father. These are the gifts he wants from us, and they give him great joy and happiness.

The idea of being gifting to the Father as our primary relationship to him negates all thoughts of acting from guilt and fear. Guilt and fear are unhappy expressions. Gifting is an expression of a happy heart. The two ways of relating could not be more different, or express more different feelings and relationships. The commandment is a commandment to relate to the

Father in joy and pleasure rather than fear and guilt. It emphasizes the truth that God is a loving heavenly Father who constantly gifts his children, and they respond by gifting him in return. Awesome!

Gifting other people with our behavior

The second commandment instructs us to change our relationships with and perceptions of other people. We are to gift them also. The many lifestyle approaches defined below are based on this foundational teaching. A heart filled up with the gifting grace of our heavenly father can naturally overflow toward the people around us. As we recognize the constant flow of gifts to us from the Father, we begin to desire to gift others in the same ways.

We normally, with the understandings of this world, relate to other people with suspicion and apprehension. We do not know what they will do. We fear that they will disrespect and disadvantage us in some way. Therefore, we defend ourselves in many ways, intending to treat them as they treat us. We become reactionary even before a reaction is called for.

Jesus commanded us to behave as God behaves toward us without regard to how we are treated by other people. We are to be gifting people no matter what happens in our lives. We gift because we are constantly receiving gifts. Those gifts fill us with joy that can be shared. The grace we receive we can give. Jesus did this very thing.

From his overflow we all received, good gift after good gift. (John 1.16)

How do we do grace to others? What kind of gifts do we give? Jesus taught many to his disciples. They are defined and discussed below. They are based on this second commandment foundation. They are expressions of *agape*, the chief characteristic of the heavenly Father.

Grace in the Message of Jesus

The law was given through Moses; grace and truth came through Jesus Christ. (John 1:17)

Grow in grace, and in an understanding of our Lord and Savior Jesus Christ. To him be glory both now and for ever. Amen. (2 Peter 3:18)

Now I commend you to God, and to the message of his grace, which is able to build you up, and to give you the inheritance among all them who are like God. (Acts 20:32)

As he passed by, he saw a man who had been blind from birth. And his disciples asked him,
"Rabbi, who sinned, this man or his parents, that he would be born blind?"
Jesus answered, "It was neither that this man sinned, nor his parents." (John 9.1-3)

Jesus lived in a world ruled by legalism. God was understood to be a legalistic God, and all of life's good and bad happenings were understood to be a payment for the good or bad behavior of the persons involved.

Legalism is an understanding of life that sees every blessing or tragedy in our lives to be caused by something we have done. Our blessings are a payoff for good behavior, and our reversals are a payoff for our bad behavior. It understands life to be a reward for obedience or disobedience to the laws of God.

God is understood to be spending most of his time passing out just rewards. He is busy punishing those who make errors, and blessing those who make none. It is understood that humans earn their experiences in life by their behavior. That is legalism.

The blind man and legalism

The passage above (John 9.1-3) is an example of the thinking of the time. Blindness was a payoff for something the man or his parents had done wrong. Otherwise, the blind man was being treated unjustly. But, God is just, so the blindness was earned by someone. Jesus said that this was not the case.

The wealthy and legalism

The opposite situation was illustrated by Jesus' statements about rich people. If a person were wealthy, he was obviously blessed by God, so he was doing what was right in the eyes of God. Wealth was a sign of the blessings of God, and poverty was a sign of his displeasure.

Jesus startled his followers when he made the following statement:

Jesus, looking around, said to his disciples, "How hard it will be for those who are wealthy to enter the kingdom of God!"
The disciples were amazed at his words.

*Jesus answered again and said to them,
"Children, how hard it is to enter the kingdom of God!
It is easier for a rope to go through the eye of a needle
than for a rich man to enter the kingdom of God."*

*They were even more astonished and said to
him, "Then who can be saved?"*

*Looking at them, Jesus said, "With people it is
impossible, but not with God; for all things are
possible with God."* (Matthew 10.23-25)

When one believes that God is controlling every
happening in life, and those happenings are both
negative and positive, one must find a system of belief
to make sense of it all. Legalism is an answer for
many people, including the religious teachers of Jesus'
day.

They understood God to be a righteous judge
who dispenses laws to be obeyed, then spends his time
rewarding persons for their performance related to
those laws. The idea was simple and easily
understood. It is logical and workable.

It was the prevailing system for human relations
also.

Legalism in personal relationships

*"You have heard that it was said, 'An eye for
an eye, and a tooth for a tooth.'* (Matthew 5.38)

This ancient teaching of Moses illustrates the
simplicity of how to relate to other people in legalistic
ways. One treats others as they are treated by them.

Legalism in human relationships simply means to treat other people as they deserve to be treated. If they treat us well, we will treat them well. If not, we will not. The Pharisees believed that when we live this way, we are behaving like God. We are living his kind of lifestyle. Other people get what they deserve from us.

The Paralytic and legalism

One day he was teaching; and there were some Pharisees and teachers of the law sitting there, who had come from every village of Galilee and Judea and from Jerusalem. The power of the Lord was present for him to perform healing.

Some men were carrying on a bed a man who was paralyzed, and they were trying to bring him in and to set him down in front of him.

Not finding any way to bring him in because of the crowd, they went up the roof and let him down through the tiles with his stretcher, into the middle of the crowd, in front of Jesus.

Seeing their faith, he said, "Friend, your sins are forgiven you."

The scribes and the Pharisees began to grumble, saying, "Who is this man who speaks blasphemies? Who can forgive sins, but God alone?"

Jesus, aware of their mumblings, answered and said to them, "Why are you reasoning in your hearts? Which is easier, to say, 'Your sins have been forgiven you,' or to say, 'Get up and walk'? So that you may understand that the Son of Man has power on earth to

free from sins,"--He said to the paralytic--"I tell you,
get up, and pick up your pallet and go home."

Immediately he got up in front of them, and
picked up what he had been lying on, and went home
giving God the glory. (Luke 5.17-25)

This story is filled with meanings just below the surface that are not always apparent to readers. Understand that the man was paralyzed because he deserved to be, in their thinking. He had sinned in some way that had led God to reward him with paralysis. He was in this condition because of his sins.

When Jesus released him from his sins, he was releasing him from the rewards for those sins. Jesus was actually canceling the payoff from God for the sins that he had committed, which in turn had caused his paralysis. Therefore, there was no longer any reason for him to be afflicted with the paralysis. He could regain his health.

Jesus' statement that the man's sins were forgiven was considered blasphemy because God is the one who had rewarded him with paralysis, so God was the only one who could cancel the reward. The theological lawyers were offended that Jesus could claim such power for himself.

Jesus then produced the result in the man that demonstrates forgiven sins. In their thinking, if he no longer continued to be paralyzed, then God must not be holding him accountable for some sin any longer. He was no longer guilty by association with his physical condition. His ability to walk showed that he was no longer guilty. His sins had been forgiven.

Jesus gifted the man with forgiveness and healing. That was the pattern of his life. He constantly gifted persons with his presence in their lives, with his patience and forgiveness, and with his healings for their bodies and spirits. He delighted in bringing joy and happiness to those in need. He was a walking demonstration of grace in the world.

Grace: the opposite of legalism

Throughout Jesus' teaching ministry, and demonstrated in his life, was seen a lifestyle that was not legalistic. Jesus taught and demonstrated grace.

Grace is a word that indicates that which is a good gift. A gift is not the same as a reward. A gift is usually unearned. It is the expression of a desire to bless from one person to another.

The teachings of Jesus are all about relationships of grace. The Sermon on the Mount (Matthew 5-7) is especially filled with actions of grace. It contains many ways to be gracious:

Go a second mile…

Turn the other cheek…

Give your cloak as well as your coat…

Pray for those who persecute you…

Return good for evil…

Forgive…

Do not judge…

Do to others as you would want…

Each of these teachings demonstrates a gifting behavior. They show persons giving good gifts of actions to persons who have not earned the treatment they are receiving. These are the "good deeds" referred to in the King James Version of the New Testament. They are good gifts. They are grace.

Jesus' actions and his teachings undercut the idea that God is simply a legalistic God. He is, rather, a gifting God of grace. He does not treat us as we deserve to be treated. He treats us better than deserved. He gifts us with blessings we do not deserve. He is a God of graciousness.

The mysterious joy factor

Usually overlooked in the concept of grace and graciousness is the presence of joy in the teachings. The Greek word *charis,* which is usually translated as grace in English, comes from a family of Greek words with interesting meanings. *Chara* means joy and *charisma* is a free gift. *Charin* means favor or blessing. All of these words have the same root meaning. They all share an emphasis on happiness and gifting.

We pick up readily on the gifting idea, but the concept of joy often eludes us. The words actually mean to give gifts of joy. They are not just any kind of gift. They are happy gifts. When John said that Jesus overflowed with grace after grace (1.16), he was actually saying that he overflowed with happy gift after happy gift. What a beautiful picture.

The pictures of Jesus shown to us by gospel writers through the events of his life paint pictures of peace, love, and joy. Jesus was a happy person and he constantly gifted persons with gifts that produced joy in them.

Powerfully, Jesus revealed that God is like him in spirit and behavior. God is constantly blessing us with gifts of happiness and joy. He is a God of gifting joy, a God of grace. How different from the pictures painted by most religions of the world. Jesus showed us a loving Father who is constantly blessing everyone with joyous gifts.

That is what grace is all about.

Agape in the Message of Jesus

Agapied *brothers, let us* agape *one another, because* agape *is of God, and everyone who does* agape *is born of God, and knows God. He who does not* agape *does not know God, because God is* agape. (1 John 4.7-8)

Now remain these three: faith, hope, and agape. *The greatest of these is* agape. *(1 Corinthians 13.13)*

"Teacher, which is the greatest commandment in the law?" And he said to him, "You shall agape *the Lord you God with all your heart, and with all your soul, and with all your mind. This is the great and first commandment. A second like it is this, you shall* agape *your neighbor as yourself. On these two commandments the whole law hangs, and the prophets."* (Matt. 22:36-40)

The New Testament Greek words *agape* and *agapao* are arguably the most pivotal words in the Jesus message. The verses above illustrate the centrality of the words in the biblical record.

The meaning of *agape* has been illusive

If the word *agape* is at the heart of the message of Jesus and the New Testament, we must understand it's meaning to understand the message. But, understanding the word has been a problem throughout Christian history.

The first official translation of the New Testament for the Christian church in the West was from the original Greek into Latin. The Roman theologian Jerome translated the Greek New Testament into Latin in the fifth century. At that time, he translated *agape* into the Latin words *charitatem* (charity) and *diligit* (love). He moved back and forth between these two words in his translation although the Greek word remained the same in all places: *agape*. Jerome obviously understood *agape* to have two differing meanings, one being charity which is a generous action, and the other the feeling of love.

The first English translation, by John Wycliffe in 1384, was based on the Latin Vulgate rather than the Greek manuscripts and followed the pattern of Jerome. Wycliffe usually translated *agape* as love, but on occasion used charity, as in 1 Corinthians 13.

One of the first English translations directly from the Greek was done by William Tyndale in the 1520s. Interestingly, he translated *agape* with the word love only. Charity was not used.

The King James Version translators reverted to Jerome and Wycliffe's approach and used both love and charity in their 1611 translation.

Today, the word charity has disappeared from modern translations. *Agape* is universally translated using the word love.

The specific meaning of the Greek word *agape* continues to be illusive. Translators know that it has shades of meaning that are not contained in the word love, but find it difficult to understand and translate those meanings. *Phileo* is the Greek word for love used in the New Testament. All English translators know this, and they know that using love to translate *agape* is not completely accurate. But knowing how to capture all of the meaning of *agape* in an English word has proven to be very difficult.

One incident in the Book of John illustrates the difference in the meaning of the two words. The resurrected Jesus visited Peter on the seashore and questioned him about his commitments and actions.

Jesus asked Peter if he loved (*agape*) him. Peter answered that he did love (*phileo*) him. Then Jesus said get busy.

Jesus asked again if Peter loved (*agape*) him. Peter answered again that he did love (*phileo*) him. Jesus again asked him to be busy with his people.

The third time Jesus asked, "Do you love (*phileo*) me Peter?" Peter was shaken by this question because it questioned his basic love for Jesus. (John 21.15-19)

Jesus and Peter were obviously using two different words with different meanings. Even though they are both translated love in English, the interplay demonstrates that they had different meanings for Jesus and Peter.

We must discover what the meaning of *agape* was in order to understand the message of the New Testament. It is the single most important word in that message.

Word meanings vary when used by differing groups of people. To discover the meanings that a group is attaching to a given word, that word must be studied in their context to see how they defined it.

How was *agape* used in New Testament passages?

We begin with the second Great Commandment: to *agape* neighbor. It is safe to conclude that this commandment is the basis for all of the other teachings of Jesus about human relationships. Neighbors are those people around us. Jesus said that we are to treat them with *agape*. Therefore, if we study his teachings about relating to other people, we should be able to draw a picture of what it means to *agape* them.

A good place to begin is the Sermon on the Mount. The three chapters in Matthew 5-7 are filled with ways of relating to the persons in our lives in many differing situations. Can we find a common behavioral thread running through these verses?

That thread appears to be a thread of unearned giftedness. Treating a neighbor as oneself is a good gift to him. He has not earned such good treatment. Also:

One mile may be required by law, but the second is a good gift.

One slapped cheek may be abuse, the second is a gift.

Forgiving seventy times seven is giving undeserved good gifts.

Praying for persons who are persecuting or despitefully using us is a gift to them.

Treating anyone better than they deserve to be treated is a good gift.

Returning good for bad is an undeserved gift.

Doing to others as we want to have done to us is a good gift.

Refusing to be judgmental is a good gift.

Based on these examples it is safe to say that *agape* refers to behavior that gives good gifts to other people. It is an action word rather than a feeling word like love. The word love barely touches the edges of its fuller meaning. The gifts given may even be given to persons who are not at all liked by the gift-giver, much less be loved by her/him. Finding an English word to capture this gift-giving idea is the challenge.

Grace and gift-giving are similar ideas

The Greek word *charis* means gift and is translated into English as "grace". The theological definition of grace is "the unmerited favor of God." If something is an unmerited favor it is an undeserved blessing. It is a good gift. That being the case, the similarity between grace and gift-giving is obvious. Treating people as Jesus taught is an exercise in grace. To *agape* persons means to gift them with unearned blessings. This understanding is different from loving a person, even though grace is one expression of love.

The emphasis of *agape* is action, not feeling. This understanding gives meaning to the exchange between Jesus and Peter above. Peter was expressing his love for the Lord, and Jesus was asking him about what he was doing for him.

If we understand that grace is the giving of unearned gifts to persons, it can provide us with a definition of *agape*. *Agape* means to "grace" other people. That is, to treat them better than they deserve, with good gifts of our behavior. A better word than love is "gracious". To be gracious within our definition of grace would mean to act with grace, or to act with graciousness.

Translating *agape* as graciousness is strange to the ear, but it does capture the meaning of the word as used by Jesus and the early Christians. It also illuminates some other concepts often used in the New Testament. Given that God is a God of grace, we understand that his Spirit is a Spirit of grace. When we are filled with the Holy Spirit, we are filled with a spirit of graciousness and joy. It is no wonder that early Christians could observe that a believer was full of the Holy Spirit. That believer was full of happy graciousness. He was constantly blessing other people with unearned blessings. He was being an *agape* person.

John was making a powerful statement when he said that God is *agape* in 1 John 4. He was saying that God is graciousness. He is a gift-giving God who constantly blesses persons regardless of their deservedness. When he says in 4.1 to test the spirits of those claiming to be spokesmen for God, we can understand the simple meaning of that saying. Persons who do not manifest graciousness and joy in their personalities are not in sync with the Living God. They do not actually know him.

A powerful truth obscured

The historic use of love to translate *agape* has robbed us of the richness of its meaning for too long. *Agape* has a far richer meaning than can be expressed in caring feelings by the word love. It defines a lifestyle that is a blessing to everyone who comes near.

No wonder the message about grace and graciousness was called "good" news. It is wonderfully good news about the gracious Spirit of God coming into persons and transforming them into persons of graciousness.

Jesus was gracious to those whom he met, whether sinners or sick. He gifted them with his care, his presence, and his healing. Not because they deserved any of this from him, but because he was full of grace.

From his fullness we have all received, grace after grace. (John 1.16)

Moses taught people how to live according to laws and commandments. Jesus taught us how to be people of grace. Moses gave us laws. Jesus gave us a new spirit of joyous grace.

The Law was given by Moses, but grace and truth came by Jesus Christ. (John 1.17)

Paul spoke of our bodies being houses for the Spirit of God. When we understand that the Spirit of God is a spirit of grace and joy, the teaching becomes even more powerful. Paul makes the point to the Galatians that laws cannot create the kind of persons being created by the indwelling Spirit of God. Only the presence of the Spirit can do that.

The fruit of the Spirit is graciousness, joy, peace, patience, kindness, goodness, dependability, gentleness, self-control. **There is no law which produces these characteristics**. (Galatians 5.22-23)

When we are possessed by the Spirit of grace, we become persons of graciousness. We become *agape* people. We constantly bless everyone whom we touch. That is *agape*.

Clothe yourselves, therefore, as chosen of God, godlike and graced with compassionate insides, kindness, humility, gentleness, tolerance, patient with one another, and forgiving each other. If anyone should have a complaint against another, just as Christ forgave you, so also you forgive. To all of these; **graciousness, which is the glue for the whole**. (Colossians 3.12-14)

Grace and *Agape*: a Message of Power

When Jesus reveals the presence of grace and graciousness in his message, he opens the door for the transformation of the spirits and lifestyles of us all. He begins a process of remaking us into people of graciousness. He is defining the Spirit of God that God is wanting to put into each of us. God wants to house his Spirit of grace in our hearts and lives. He wants us to become like he and his Son.

Let this way of believing that was in Christ Jesus be in you also. (Philippians 2.5)

Grace found many expressions in the teachings and life demonstrations of Jesus. He was constantly showing how this gift-giving, happy spirit was lived out daily in our lives. He knew that when we understand his message of graciousness, we can begin to have the spirit of grace in us. Our lives begin to become reoriented and remade. They begin to experience a fullness that we have not known.

The key to all of this transformation is the content of what we believe about God, about ourselves, and about how to live life. Jesus revealed many truths about all of these subjects. His truths become the object of our beliefs that can change us completely, in spirit and behavior.

Part Three: Content of the Jesus Message

What is the content of this powerful, life-changing message of Jesus? What specific truths did he reveal to the world? What revelations did he make that are so monumental?

The message is the content of the teachings and demonstrations of Jesus in the writings of Matthew, Mark, Luke, and John. Those many experiences and teachings adhere to certain themes important to Jesus. He was teaching and living out his message from the Father.

Certain themes can be detected. They may be deduced from the many episodes, specific revelations, and teachings. Our conclusions about some of those are found below. The subjects are not exhaustive of all that Jesus shared. But, hopefully, they represent the most basic elements of his message to humanity.

In it all, one must decide if he/she can accept and believe the message of Jesus or not. If one believes, a change in mindset and understanding follows. The way one views life and God's role in it changes. The understanding about who God is and how he is relating to humanity will become different.

Additionally, one must buy into the lifestyle teachings of Jesus. He was radically different in his approach to behavior. If one can accept his approach and live it out in daily life, everything changes.

The change reality is why the apostles spoke of *metanoia*. The Greek word is usually translated as "repentance" in English. But it literally means to change one's mind or thinking. It means to change what one believes. This in turn leads to changes in behavior and lifestyle. An unwillingness to change one's thinking makes belief impossible, and therefore, does not result in a changed spirit and lifestyle.

The Message of Jesus about Who We Are

Jesus revealed many things about who we are and what is our condition in life. He said that he had come because our condition is deadly destructive and God loves us too much to leave us to our own devices.

Jesus gave us some bad news about our condition and always pointed toward the good news of what God hopes for us. He said that we are the living dead but that the Father wants us to have life that overflows in joy and fullness. He came so that we might have a quality of life that was beyond our reach without his help. Here is what he revealed. Here is his message to us about us.

1. We Believe the Wrong Realities

I am who I believe I am. You are who I believe you are. God is who I believe he is. That which is valuable is what I believe to be valuable. What is right is what I believe to be right.

We live life according to our beliefs. Our beliefs actually control our lives. Our beliefs cause us to be optimistic or pessimistic. They cause us to think well of ourselves or disrespect ourselves. They determine what we think to be right or wrong. They cause us to feel responsible for ourselves or to expect others to care for us. What we believe is powerful in the functioning of our lives.

We believe certain things about God and what he does. We believe certain things about ourselves and our ways of living. We believe certain things about people and the ways they are and the ways they will behave. All of these beliefs impact our daily living. They contribute to our lives or they detract from our lives. They build up our lives or they tear down our lives.

If our beliefs are inaccurate to reality, we are in deep trouble. We are living lives of fantasy. If they are erroneous, our living may be disastrous. That which we believe will give us full and satisfying lives may actually be robbing us of our lives.

What we believe may be the single most important aspect of our lives when measuring happiness and fullness.

Jesus encountered faulty beliefs from the very beginning of his ministry. They were probably the subject of the discussions between the twelve year old Jesus and the rabbis. Later, he was constantly disagreeing with the Pharisees, lawyers, and scribes. Their understanding of God and his will was at odds with his knowledge. Their beliefs about how to measure and treat people were radically different than his. He rejected the lifestyle they taught and promoted. He said that their beliefs were killing their lives.

Beliefs direct behavior

Jesus said that what a person says and does are reflections of what he believes:

"A good man from out of the good treasure of his heart expresses that which is good. An evil man out of the evil treasure expresses that which is evil. His mouth speaks out of the overflow of his heart." (Jesus in Luke 6.45)

In the ancient world, the heart was the seat of understanding and belief. The stomach or bowels were the seats of emotion. When Jesus said that what is in a person's heart expresses itself in his speech and behavior, he is talking about what that person believes. Our beliefs express themselves in our behavior.

In addition, the heart is the source of the spirit that we manifest in our lives. It is the seat of joy or sadness, optimism or pessimism, peace or fear, and care or coldness. From our hearts come the attitudes that we live out. If our heart is good, our spirit is good. If our heart is bad, our spirit is bad also.

We are being destroyed by deadly erroneous beliefs

Jesus revealed and taught that our lives are missing the mark because our understandings and beliefs miss the mark.

Jesus answered, "Truly, I say to you, everyone who practices error[6] is a slave to error. A slave does not live in the house forever, but the son lives there forever. If then the son should set you free, you shall be truly free." (Jesus in John 8.34-36)

Jesus taught that our basic problem in living life is that we are enslaved by misunderstanding, misguided behavior, and destructive lifestyles. Our beliefs are destructively wrong, and we need to be set free from those beliefs.

The power of wrong beliefs can be disastrous. Our most basic beliefs are not simply intellectual. They have deadly consequences for our living and our relationship with God.

So Jesus said to those Judeans who believed in him, "If you live by my teachings, you are truly my disciples. You shall know the truth, and the truth shall set you free." (Jesus in John 8.31-32)

---

[6] The Greek word *hamartia* is almost always translated as "sin" in the New Testament by English translators. This is done in spite of the fact that it has many synonyms. The correct word to be used of the many synonyms is determined by the context in which the word is found. In this case, Jesus is talking about truth. The opposite of truth is error.

Jesus was constantly speaking about the truth. He said that he was revealing the truth to the world, and that truth could change life. He spoke constantly of having a message[7] from God which gives life to those who believe it because it reveals the truth. (John 5.24-25)

Life comes from believing Jesus

English translators often confuse the biblical verses that make this point by saying that we are to believe "on" Jesus. We are actually to believe in Jesus and in his revelations and teachings. We cannot separate who he is from his revelations. He lived his message, and that message sets us free to be whom God wants us to be.

The New Testament writers constantly emphasized belief as the secret to life. Belief in Jesus and his teachings make it possible for us to have the Spirit and life of God in us. Through believing we begin to think like God thinks and behave like God behaves. We begin to have the life of the heavens and of eternity. We become spiritual offspring of the Heavenly Father.

---

[7] Message is a better English translation of the Greek word *logos* than is "word." Word must be further defined to be understandable. Message points us immediately to the content of what Jesus did and said.

Those who did accept him, he gave to them the power to be offspring of God, to those who believe in his name. (John 1.12)

Believing the wrong things robs us of the fullness of life

Jesus said that believing the wrong things is our actual condition. We have been lied to and deceived, and we have believed the lies. We believe the lies about God, about other people, about ourselves, and about how to live life. We are people who have been imprisoned by falseness and fantasy and our lives are being destroyed by the falseness. (See John 8.31forward)

Jesus referred to us as dead people. We are the walking, living dead. We are not alive to the degree God intends for us to be because we are trapped in beliefs that take the life out of us. We become satisfied with life that is far less than we are meant to have. Paul stated this fact in his letter to the Romans:

All have missed the mark and are less than the wonderfulness of God. (Romans 3.23)

Jesus came to set us free from that which is killing us, and to give us understandings that give us life. He revealed the truth about God, about us, and about living. And the truth is wonderfully life-giving. We must only believe it to receive the life he has planned for us.

Jesus addressed numerous beliefs that are common to all persons. These beliefs destroy the fullness of life that everyone is pursuing. They are beliefs that are promoted by the "world".

God is legalistic and harsh in his punishments.

I am less important than other people.

I should treat people exactly as they deserve to be treated.

I should take care of number one however necessary.

My goals justify the means I use to reach them.

No one is really honest.

I should destroy my competitors.

I should be one of the bunch in values and behavior.

I allow my sex drive to have free expression.

Possessions determine my value in society.

Leadership positions give my life superior value.

Always repay hurts done to me by others.

Never forget a wrong done to me or a favor done to me.

Criticize mistakes in persons in order to bring about change in them.

Be in competition with everyone.

Tomorrow is filled with fears.

We must change our beliefs in order to have real life

The Greek word *metanoia* is universally translated into English as "repentance." Repentance means to feel sorry for or guilty for past wrongs. But the emphasis of the Greek word *metanoia* means to change our thinking or understanding, to change our minds. It is used in the New Testament to mean to change our beliefs.

God cannot set us free from missing the mark if we will not change our ways of thinking and believing. We are trapped in lies and deceptions and cannot escape them if we will not believe differently. Believing in Jesus is the key to new life. Jesus revealed, taught, and demonstrated the truth. If we will believe in him and what he has shown us, we can become "new creations in Christ." We can experience his promise of overflowing life.

"I have come that you may have life and have it to the overflow." (Jesus in John 10.10)

Beliefs are the key. Believing a lie robs us of life. Believing the truth gives us life. Jesus is "the way, the truth, and the life."

What are these life-giving truths that Jesus revealed? We must find them, believe them, and have life.

"The lamp of the body is the eye. Therefore, if your eye is healthy, your whole body will be full of

light. But if your eye is defective, your whole body will be full of darkness. Therefore, if the light that is in you is darkness, how great is the darkness!" (Jesus in Matthew 6.22-23)

Beliefs give life or take life

He has made you to become alive, who were dead in destructive living and misguided beliefs.[8] (Ephesians 2.1)

Beliefs and their resultant behavior either build life up or tear life down. Understanding nurtures happiness and satisfaction or does just the opposite. Beliefs and understandings have great affect on the life of every person alive. We are all very aware of the differing ways and understandings of persons around us. We are delighted with some and dismayed with others. Persons see life through their own perceptions and understandings and that has great influence on their attitudes and behavior.

We are often frustrated with the way others perceive situations when their perception is different than ours. Especially, when their perceptions produce negative and unhappy experiences when we think there is no real cause for such understandings.

We are aware that two persons can live through the same experience and each view its meaning and significance very differently. The beliefs of each are

---

[8] See Appendix 3, Trespasses and Sins.

different. Those differences determine the effects of the experience in the life of each.

As an example, two young couples have lost a child in a tragic death. One is angry with God because he caused or allowed the death to take place. They experience an ongoing hurt and bitterness. The other experiences a closer and more meaningful walk with God because his presence and assurance helped them through the tragedy. That presence and its support has them on the road to recovery. What each believed about God and his actions controlled their differing responses. Their beliefs made the difference.

Jesus taught that the world is filled with inaccurate and destructive beliefs that rob persons of life. His revelations and teachings cut through those deceptions and help people to know the truth, and that truth sets them free from the life- and spirit-killing lies that they have believed. (John 8.31ff)

Jesus described persons as the living dead. He referred to people around him as being dead people.

*Jesus said to him, "Follow me, **and leave the dead to bury their own dead."** * (Matthew 8.22)

They were dead simply because they were not alive to the degree that God intends for them to be. They were missing the fullness of life because of their deadly beliefs and destructive behavior. Jesus said that he and his message could give persons a new kind of life. The life he promised is beautifully filling and satisfying.

"The thief only comes to steal, kill, and destroy.
I came that you may have life and may have it to the
overflow.*"* (Jesus in John 10.10)

Jesus answered her, "Everyone who drinks this
water will thirst again, but whoever will drink the
*water which I will give **him shall in no way thirst***
***forever.** The water which I will give him shall become*
a spring of water in him, surging up into eternal life."
(John 4.13-14)

What awesome promises! But to realize them,
persons must believe in Jesus and his teachings. They
must learn to see life, people and the world through his
eyes. They must change their thinking and
understanding about God, people, and behavior. They
must stop believing in old ways and begin to think in
new ways. When this happens, persons become new
kinds of persons with new spirits and new lifestyles.
They become new creations. They become like the
Father and the Son. They become heavenly, eternal
people: "saints".

"Make them godly by means of the truth; your
message is truth." (Jesus to God, John 17.17)

In keeping with his will, he birthed us again by
the message of truth, so that we would be a kind of
first edition among his creations. (James 1.18)

"It is the spirit that gives life. The flesh profits nothing. The words that I speak to you, they are spirit, and they are life." (Jesus in John 6:63)

What persons believe controls how they understand and live life. If their beliefs are wrong, living can be misguided. Jesus taught that this is indeed the human condition. Persons are believing the wrong things and living lives that are not really alive. Their beliefs are killing their spirits and therefore their joy and fullness. He came to change that situation in everyone who will believe his message.

2. We can Change in Spirit, Personality, and Lifestyle

Jesus answered him, "Truly I say to you, unless a person has been born from above, he cannot recognize the kingdom of God." (John 3.3)

I encourage you, brethren, by means of the kind helps of God, to present your bodies a living sacrifice, holy, approved by God, which is your spiritual service. Do not be molded by the ways of this world. Be changed by the renewing of your thinking, so that you may demonstrate that which is the good and acceptable and whole will of God. (Romans 12.1-2)

Change takes place when we begin to believe the message of Jesus and make it a part of our lives. The change in spirit and life takes place after we change our thinking and understanding about God, people, and life.

The New Testament speaks often of an experience translated by the word "repentance". The Greek word is *metanoia*, which means to change one's thinking, understanding, or beliefs. It is the experience of beginning to believe differently than before. It is tied to the revelations and teachings of Jesus. When we believe what Jesus has revealed and taught, it leads to a change in belief and thinking.

Belief that God is an angry, legalistic God affects our spirits and outlook about life and living.

When we begin to understand and accept that God is a happy, gracious God, our minds and spirits begin to change because of that belief. We begin to have a different attitude and lifestyle. His happiness becomes our happiness and his graciousness becomes our graciousness. His Spirit begins to overcome our spirits so that we become more like him. We are being reborn, born from above.

...saying, "The time is fulfilled, and the kingdom of God is at hand: change your thinking and believe in the good message." (Mark 1.15)

A major part of the message of Jesus was about our present circumstances as persons, and how God wants to change those circumstances. He had much to say about worldly deceptions, misguided lives, destructive behavior, and brainwashed understandings.

Jesus was on a mission to change our condition from death to life in the here and now. Regrettably, many Christians believe that his teachings mostly refer to the afterlife. This is a popular idea among many because it releases them from attempting to make more of this life. It accepts the inevitable evils of this world and focuses on the wonder of heaven. This is regrettable because it robs lives of what God has for us in the here and now.

Jesus said that he had come to make a difference in this life. He spoke of overflowing abundance in living. We would assume that such is an automatic characteristic of Heaven, so for him to work at it here meant that the overflow is here and now.

At the end of the Sermon on the Mount, after three chapters of life teachings, Jesus said this,

"Every one who hears these teachings of mine, and does not practice them, shall be seen as a foolish man who built his house on sand. The rain fell, and the floods came, and the winds blew and pounded that house; and it fell: and great was its fall." (Matthew 7.24-26)

Jesus came to make a difference in life today, tomorrow, and the next day. He was making a difference in people, their understandings, and their behavior in the present. He was setting people free from life-robbing understandings, behavior, emotions, and lifestyles.

The New Testament refers to the new life that Jesus gave to persons as "eternal life". It is life like that of the heavens. It is God's kind of life. It begins now and goes on forever. It is an answer to Jesus' request in the Model Prayer that the will of God be done on Earth as it is in Heaven.

Theologians have had difficulty accepting this emphasis as being about this life rather than the life of the hereafter. Mainly because the life teachings of Jesus appear to be unreasonable for everyday living.

For example, to forgive a person seventy times seven is a very impractical way of living in daily life. Many think that he must have been talking about life in his kingdom after his return. But we cannot escape the references of Jesus and his disciples to the lifestyle of persons in the present.

God loves his world. He said it is very good. But, it has been led astray by a spirit that destroys life and people. Jesus came to set it free, one person at a time. His message does that, when understood and believed. When we change our thinking and believe what he reveals and teaches, we begin to become different persons with a different spirit and lifestyle. We begin to become alive.

3. Jesus Came to Give us Overflowing Hearts and Lives

We have lost our spirits. We have become controlled by spirits that do not fill us with life. In fact, they destroy life within us.

Life comes from unselfishness. We have become possessed with a selfish spirit.

Life comes from truthfulness. We have become possessed with a deceptive spirit.

Life comes from peacefulness. We have become possessed with an anxious spirit.

Life comes from control of self. We are out of control with a spirit of confusion.

Life comes with trusting. We do not trust.

Things do not give life. We treasure things most of all.

Life comes with self-respect. In its absence, we pursue respect from others first.

Life comes with hope. We have lost hope and optimism.

The spirit that reigns in the world is a spirit that destroys life. When we are possessed by it, it takes the joy and fullness out of our lives. Jesus came to break the power of that spirit in us, and replace it with the Spirit of God.

Jesus often referred to the adversarial spirit of the world. That spirit is constantly luring us to be persons without life. He used the words Satan and Devil to identify its personality and presence. The two terms were used interchangeably in the New Testament as evidenced in the testing of Jesus on the mountain in Matthew:

*Again, the **Devil** took him to a very high mountain, and showed him all of the kingdoms of the world, and the majesty of them. And he said to him, "All these things will I give you, if you will fall down and worship me."*

*Then Jesus said to him, "Get away from me, **Satan**. Because it is written, 'You shall worship the Lord your God, and him only shall you serve.'"* (Matthew 4.8-10)

This adversarial spirit is a spirit that destroys spirit and life. It is a killing spirit that can ensnare persons with false thinking that then leads to destructive thinking and behavior. Jesus called these ways of thinking and acting lies and deceptions.

"Why do you not understand my message? Because you are unable to hear my teachings. You are offspring of a destructive father, and the drives of your father you want to pursue. He was a killer from the beginning, and did not stand for truth, because truth is not in him. Whenever he speaks falsely, he speaks from himself, because he is a liar and the father of liars. And because I speak the truth, you do not believe me." (John 8.43-45)

Interestingly, this passage in John paints a picture of persons who are "brainwashed" by lies and deceptions. They have been deceived for so long by the lies of the Great Deceiver that they can no longer hear the truth when it is presented to them. Their beliefs and understandings are wrong and are enslaving their lives with destructive thinking and living.

Jesus promised to set them free from their enslavement to wrong, error, and deception.

So Jesus said to those Judeans who believed in him, "If you live by my teachings, you are truly my disciples. You shall know the truth, and the truth shall set you free." (John 8.31-32)

The world is filled with this spirit of lies and deceptions. It has great power because it destroys persons and lives. Sin is sin because it destroys life. It wars against that which gives life. It causes persons to be dead in wrong understanding and wrong living. Our spirits and lives cease to be alive to all that God intends for them.

Jesus came to change all of that.

"The thief only comes to steal, kill, and destroy. I came that you may have life and may have it to the overflow." (John 10.10)

When we believe that the adversarial spirit is part of our world, we can be sensitive to the guiding presence of God in our lives. We learn to discern deceptive and destructive situations and know how deadly they can be to us. We recognize their presence in the lives of those around us and help as we may. We no longer walk blindly through our lives and never understand that God is trying to guide us in the ways of life. We develop wisdom about life and its consequences, and we choose his life and his consequences. When we believe.

An awesome part of Jesus' teachings was the wonderfulness of the kind of life he instructed us to have. The New Testament writers used the word "glorious" to describe it. The word has many synonyms: wonderful, praiseworthy, beautiful, happy, joyous, and so on. The Jesus lifestyle is a blessing to everyone involved with it; those who live it and those who are touched by it.

Paul would say later that by default our lives are less than God has intended for them to be,

...everyone has missed the mark and come short of the wonderfulness of God. (Romans 3.23)

We are all deficient when it comes to knowing how to live life, and in experiencing the life that God intends for us. Jesus came to correct that situation. His teachings lead us to life.

Too often our lives are possessed by selfishness, guilt, fear, anger, hate, and suspicion. When this is true, fullness of life flees. None of these emotions give life to us. They destroy life in us.

The revelations and teachings of Jesus will provide the ways for us to escape the destructive understandings and emotions that enslave us. They will attack the causes of guilt, anger, and fear. They can bring peace and freedom to the spirit.

Jesus came to help dead people come to life

Jesus called us dead in our messed up beliefs and wrong lifestyles.

He has made you to become alive, who were dead in wrong living and destructive thinking. (Ephesians 2.1)

Jesus wants us to have the life that God has intended for everyone since the time of creation itself. Strangely, most people are dead and do not know that life is available to them. They do not know that they have options. They are bound up with beliefs and behavior that is killing their spirits and hearts and they do not understand what is going on.

God had to send Jesus to give clues to the clueless. Paul believed that inside of every person there is a voice that sounds life's cautions and discontents. We know that all is not right. What we do not know is what to do next. We have to have help with that. The Father sent Jesus to teach us his ways and infuse us with his Spirit.

Life can be glorious

The reason the life described and lived out by Jesus is called glorious is because it is so blessed in its spirit and expression. Persons who live the way Jesus taught are wonderful people. They embody the convictions and values that make life inspiring, honorable, dignified, and noble. They are truly light and salt to their world. They bless everyone whom they touch. They are a glorious kingdom of people who serve a king who is even more glorious.

Our world desperately needs the presence of people with the Spirit of God in all of its affairs. It hungers for right and good in the midst of so much hate, deception, and destruction. Christians can be lights in the darkness just as he was light in the darkness.

When we believe that God has more for us than we can ever possess on our own, we begin the journey to abundant life. When we believe that "this is all there is", we frustrate his efforts. We must believe in order to receive.

The mystery of fullness and peace

The many laws about daily life proclaimed by the scribes, Pharisees, and religious lawyers around Jesus were designed to produce the best of living. They were designed to prevent persons from behaving in ways that hurt or destroy life. After all, everyone was pursuing satisfying and happy lives. The question was and still is: What produces happiness, and conversely, what destroys happiness?

How can we find out the effects of certain kinds of believing and behaving? How do we really know what takes from life and what builds up life? Jesus acknowledged that the answers were difficult to find.

"Enter in through the narrow gate: because the gate is wide, and the road is broad which leads to destruction, and they are many who travel that way. But the gate is narrow, and the road is straight, which leads to [abundant] life, and they are few who find it." (Jesus in Matthew 7.13-14)

Jesus came to reveal the life that is God's kind of life and lifestyle. He knew that we could seldom find the right answers for ourselves. We need help. We need for God to help us find real life. We must trust and believe in Jesus and his teachings in order to find the overflowing life that God has for us.

Many of the teachings of Jesus are often considered impractical and idealistic. They are often discounted and ignored. But, life can be found in them. When believed, understood, and practiced, life begins to become full to overflowing.

The difference is belief. What we believe influences how we act. When our beliefs become those of Jesus, our lives begin to become like God intends for them to be. They begin to become heavenly or holy.

Our lives are controlled by our beliefs about living, relating to other persons, ourselves, and God. If our beliefs are wrong or off base, they rob us of the fullness of life. If they are true to reality, they fill our lives up with meaning and joy.

The writer of the Book of Hebrews spends all of chapter eleven discussing the power of belief in our lives. He does a litany of historic people of faith. The beginning of numerous verses in chapter eleven begin with "by faith…" in most English Bibles. More clearly they should be translated into English as "because of belief…". The persons mentioned behaved certain ways because of what they believed. They acted out of beliefs that led to blessings.

Without belief it is impossible to please him [God]. He who comes to God must believe that he is, and that he gives to those who search for him. (Hebrews 11.6)

4. Jesus is Creating the Life of God in Persons

Life is in him; and the life is the enlightening of mankind. (John 1.4)

Just as the Father has life in himself; so he has given to the Son to have life in himself; (John 5.26)

We can be committed to becoming more and more like the Father in mindset and behavior. We can learn to have eternal life, life like that of God and his heavens.

The spirit and life that is God's is a wonderful experience. Far from just getting a person into heaven, it transforms life in persons in the here and now. It begins now and lasts forever.

The Gospels are filled with the teachings of Jesus that describe eternal life. All of those teachings of his about how to live are patterned after the life and spirit of God. They are the ways in which God goes about his life and work. They are the lifestyle of the eternal.

The surprise of it all is that every one of the qualities of spirit and life revealed by Jesus is marvelous. To be a person who is gracious, joyous, forgiving, caring, peacemaking, uncritical, kind and loving is really more than anyone can ask of a person. But that is exactly the kind of person whom God is, whom Jesus is, and whom God wants us to be.

Jesus revealed, demonstrated and taught an otherworldly lifestyle

A lifestyle that is patterned after the values and attitudes of this world is a deficient and deadly lifestyle. It is deficient in that it does not build spirit and fill up life with meaning, peace and power. In the extreme, it does just the opposite. It robs life of spirit and power.

Jesus said that we must be born from above, from outside of this world, in order to have real life. In order to have this experience, our understandings and beliefs must change from those common to ordinary life. We must be open to what God is seeking to do with us. We must expect his presence in us to change our thinking and our lifestyles.

"Do not be perplexed that I said to you that it is necessary for you to be born from above. The wind blows where it chooses and you hear its sound, but do not know from where it comes and where it goes. The same is true of everyone who has been born of the Spirit." (John 3.7-8)

Jesus said that the means by which God transforms our thinking and behaving is the presence of his spirit within us. God is spirit and he is a distinctive kind of spirit. His spirit has distinctive traits and those traits were revealed to us through Jesus. His teachings were constantly defining the type of spirit and behavior that is that of God.

The presence of God attends the understanding and acceptance of the teachings of Jesus. When a person realizes that Jesus is communicating God to us, and begins to understand and believe what he revealed, that person begins the process of change to become like the Father and the Son in spirit and lifestyle.

Therefore, if any man is in Christ, he is a new creation. The old ways have passed away. Behold, they have become new. (2 Corinthians 5.17)

By his own will he brought us forth by means of the message of truth, so that we might be a kind of first editions of his creations. (James 1.18)

The finished product is intended to be marvelous

What kind of persons are created by the presence of the spirit of God and the teachings of Jesus? The first believers were astounded by what they experienced and observed. Persons changed in delightful ways.

The fruit of the Spirit is graciousness, joy, peace, patience, kindness, goodness, dependability, gentleness, self-control. There are no laws that can produce these things. (Galatians 5.22-23)

Selfish people become gracious to those around them.
Unhappy people become joyous.

There is a change in spirit and personality for everyone who understands, accepts, and believes.

The list can go on based on the many teachings of Jesus. Persons become forgiving, generous, non-judgmental, constructive and caring. All in all, the kind of person created by the teachings of Jesus and the presence of the spirit of God is a fabulous person.

The result is a life of fullness and power

The Jesus kind of life and lifestyle fills life up with happiness and meaning. Abundant life is not found in the lifestyle common to the world at large. It is not found in possessions, powerful positions, or celebrity. Persons may have all of these things and miss out on real and full life. Other persons may have none of these things and have overflowing lives. That is the true mystery of living. It is knowing what produces life and what destroys life. Jesus came that we might find those answers and have life.

Persons can be alive and yet dead.

The Message of Jesus About the God of Grace and Joy

The Good News About God

A foundational revelation to us by Jesus was his revelation of the person and workings of God. He addressed the questions about the personality and activity of the Living God. The mystery of who God is and what he is doing has been a mystery among humans throughout their existence. Jesus came to both teach and demonstrate who God really is and how he behaves toward us.

God, having in times past spoken to our ancestors through the prophets, in various fragments and by various means, has in these last days spoken to us in his Son, whom he appointed the receiver of all things, through whom also he made the age; **who being the brightness of his glory, and the very image of his character**, *and under girding all these things with his powerful message, when he had cleansed us from 'missing the mark', sat down on the right hand of the Majesty on high. Having become so much better than other messengers, so that he has received a name more excellent than they.* (Hebrews 1.1-4)

Jesus is the spiritual offspring of God. He is God's Son in spirit, attitude, lifestyle, values, and behavior. He acts like God. He shows us God by his own personality and lifestyle.

*Philip said to him, "Lord, show us the Father, and that will satisfy us." Jesus said to him, "Have I been with you all this time, and you do not understand me, Philip? **He who has seen me has seen the Father**. How can you say, show us the Father?"*
(John 14.8-9)

No one has seen God at any time. The only born Son, who is in the bosom of the Father, he has revealed him. (John 1:18)

Jesus opens the windows of heaven so that we may see inside. He shows us the personality of God. He shows us the ways in which God treats persons on Earth. He shows us what God deems important in life. He is the living Emmanuel, God with us.

The revelations of Jesus are unique among all of the religious understandings throughout history. Religions have always been a part of the human experience, evidently. Each religion has attempted to speak for the divine and eternal and explain deities and their workings. But, Jesus reveals to us a God whom we have never known from any other source.

The personality and behavior that Jesus demonstrated by his own life is not what any religion expected. In fact, many Christians today cannot fully accept the revelations shown to us by Jesus. Jesus does not philosophically fit their understanding of who God must be if he is truly God. They have their ideas and definitions and Jesus often disagrees with those notions. So they find ways to discount what he said and what he demonstrated. But, the Bible is very clear on this point,

"I have revealed you to the men whom you have given to me from the world. They were yours and you have given them to me, and they have observed your teachings. Now they know all that you have given to me are from you. I have given to them all of the teachings which you have given to me, and they have accepted them, and know honestly that I came from you, and they believe that you did send me with your message." (Jesus to the Father in John 17.6-8)

What were these demonstrations and teachings that Jesus brought from God to us? What did he show us that is so unusual about God? There are many characteristics of God that he showed us, a few are treated below. They are significant revelations that impact our understanding of God and his ways. In so doing, they impact the ways in which we fellowship with him, understand him to be working in our lives, and understand his expectations for us.

1. God is Personal

"Are not five sparrows sold for two coins? Not one of them is overlooked in the sight of God. The very hairs of your head are all numbered. Do not be afraid. You are more valuable than many sparrows." (Jesus in Luke 12.6-7)

"Therefore, do not be like them, because your Father knows what things you need before you ask him." (Jesus in Matthew 6.8)

"Even so, I say to you, there is joy in the presence of the angels of God over one sinner who turns around." (Jesus in Luke 15.10)

In a world of distant gods and impersonal deities, the message of Jesus about the person of God became more personal than anyone had ever thought. Ancient gods were gods of nations and races. Their first concerns were with the health and wealth of peoples and nations. Secondarily they may be interested in individual persons. But not many were concerned with individuals at all.

Jesus revealed God to be very personal with concern for every person alive. Jesus showed little interest in nations, races and societies. He was consumed with the plight of individuals. He wanted each of us to have a kind of life that only God can help us find. It is a life that is filled to overflowing with grace, joy, power, and peace.

2. God is a God of Grace Rather than Legalism

The teachings of Jesus and the parables he told which illustrate the basic nature and behavior of God play grace against legalism. Legalism identifies a nature and behavior that fixes laws and insists that persons live according to those laws. When one keeps the laws, they are blessed by God. When they violate the laws, they are punished by God. Life is lived according to numerous laws of life.

The religious world in which Jesus lived, both Jewish and pagan, was a very legalistic world. God was to be feared terribly because he was always on the verge of anger and retribution. Because humans can never perfectly keep laws, guilty verdicts were always being rendered for them. Guilt was an everpresent way of life. The laws constantly proved how imperfect and inadequate every person is who is alive.

Legalism was compounded by the understanding that every happening in life is a payoff from either keeping or breaking the laws. Wealth was a payoff by God for righteousness. Tragedy was a payoff for missing the mark. The following passage from John demonstrates the understanding of New Testament persons about what causes tragedy in peoples' lives.

While passing, he saw a man who had been blind from birth. His disciples asked him, "Teacher, who sinned, this man or his parents that he should be born blind?"

Jesus answered, "Neither this man sinned nor his parents. But so that the activity of God may be demonstrated in him, I must do the works of him who sent me while it is still day. Night is coming when no one is able to work. While I am in the world, I am the light of the world." (John 9.1-5)

The disciples knew that someone did something wrong to make the blind man deserve to be blind. God would not allow him to be blind otherwise. Jesus disagreed. He said that the blindness was not caused by the sins of the man or his parents. His idea went against all contemporary thinking of the day. Everyone knew that a legalistic God always pays just desserts to those who have earned them. Blindness was someone's just dessert.

Jesus played with this idea when he healed the palsied man who was lowered through the roof. Since religious leaders believed that his palsy was caused by sins that he had committed, release from those sins would remove the reason for his physical maladies.

"Which is easier, to say to the one sick with a palsy, your sins are forgiven; or to say, get up, pick up your bed, and walk?" So that you may know that the Son of man has the power on earth to free from sins, he said to the sick with palsy,

"I say to you, get up, pick up your bed, and go to your house."

He got up and immediately picked up the bed, and went out in front of them all; so that they were all astounded, and praised God, saying, "We have never seen anything like this." (Mark 2.9-12)

The fact that the man no longer suffered from the palsy meant that he was no longer guilty of the sins that caused the palsy. No matter which act Jesus did, forgiving sin or healing the man, the results were the same in their thinking.

That is the way legalism worked. If a person sinned he would receive tragedy as a reward. If a person was receiving blessings, it was sign that he was living legally.

This legalistic idea came into play later when Jesus said,

It is easier for a rope[9] to go through a needle's eye, than it is for a rich man to enter the kingdom of God. (Mark 10.25)

Everyone knew that wealthy people were pleasing God or they would not be blessed by him with wealth. Jesus was going against their basic beliefs by putting down legalism as the way in which God works with people.

---

[9] The use of camel in this verse is a misunderstanding by Greeks of the meaning of the Aramaic word *gamla*. Jesus probably taught in Aramaic and *gamla* in Aramaic means rope. *Kamelon* in Greek means camel in English. The Greek speakers misunderstood what Jesus was saying because of the language difference.

Jesus did not stop with refuting their ideas about a legalistic God, he revealed how God does behave. He introduced a God of grace.

The law was given by Moses, but grace and truth came by Jesus Christ. (John 1.17)

The concept of grace used in the New Testament is illustrated in the copy above. It is the active blessing of persons who may or may not have earned a blessing. Jesus revealed God as one who is overflowing with grace toward everyone on Earth. John said of Jesus,

We all received from his overflowing, grace after grace. (John 1.16)

Jesus taught many parables illustrating God as being gracious rather than legalistic. The Prodigal Son (Luke 15), the man who hired workers all during the day (Matthew 20), and his injunction to be like the Father as persons of grace,

"You have heard that it was said, 'You shall be gracious to your neighbor, and despise your enemy.' But I tell you, be gracious to your enemies, and pray for those who persecute you; so that you may be offspring of your Father who is in heaven: because he makes his sun to rise on the bad and the good, and sends rain on the just and the unjust." (Matthew 5.43-45)

This revelation is phenomenal. No religion has ever revealed God to be a God of grace. God is always understood to be a god of laws and legalisms. He hands down laws and then judges persons and nations according to those laws. He then rewards on the basis of his judgments. He blesses the observant and punishes the transgressors. This is his role in the world. He is a legalistic god who deals with humanity in legalistic ways.

Some have revealed God as practicing grace on occasion, but grace is the exception to his ordinary behavior. Jesus disagreed. He painted a picture of God in his teachings, and in his demonstrations of the Father in his own life, as a God of grace by nature and operation. If this is true, it is marvelous good news. It means that God is not treating us as we deserve at any time.

Sacrifices are legalistic

The sacrificial systems practiced by ancient religions, Judaism included, were based on legalism. The sacrifices provided means for escaping guilty judgments from the gods. No one could keep all the laws and please the gods, so everyone was guilty and in need of punishment.

Sacrifices were prescribed to offset deserved punishments. They provided a way to "balance the books". This whole system was brought about by legalistic understandings of how the gods behave toward humans. The gods were gods of laws who rendered guilty verdicts for everyone. Therefore, everyone had to make sacrifices to escape the deserved punishments of the gods.

When Jesus revealed that God is actually a God of grace rather than legalisms, he undercut the sacrificial system practiced in the Temple at Jerusalem. The Pharisees and lawyers around him understood this perfectly. Jesus was saying that the Temple and its sacrifices were not needed to please God.

He reinforced this with the woman at the Samaritan well when he told her that location was of no concern to God. Worship of him is spiritual rather than physical. Physical sacrifices and geographical locations were unimportant to the Father. In Amos 5 and Isaiah 1 those prophets had said the same thing. The spirit and behavior of persons was more important than Temple ceremonies.

The implications of grace are astounding. If God is a God of grace as Jesus revealed, religious practice is totally changed. Legalistic understandings are inaccurate and untrue. They are part of the lies that imprison people with ideas, understandings, and behavior that is hugely burdensome. No wonder Jesus thought that we need rest from all of that.

"Put my yoke upon you, and learn from me. I am gentle and humble in heart, and you will find rest for your souls. My yoke fits and my burden is light." (Jesus in Matthew 11.29-30)

Grace makes the difference.

3. God is our Heavenly Father

Jesus addressed God as "our Father." He told stories of fathers who were representative of God. He shared teachings that portrayed God relating to us as a good father relates to his children.

"Call no man on Earth your father, because only one is your Father, even he who is in heaven." (Jesus in Matthew 23.9)

To understand God's relationship to us as that of a parent rather than a judge is Earth-shattering. Parents relate to their children in ways more wonderful than anyone else who knows them.

Parents want the best for their children regardless of their shortcomings.

Parents help their children overcome failure in life. Parents pick children up, dust them off, and help them to get on with life.

Parents are forgiving because they are committed to the success of their children more than their judgment.

Parents provide for their children.

Parents understand the weakness and strengths of their children.

Parents watch their children grow and develop with joy and satisfaction.

Parents train and educate their children.

Jesus always addressed God as his father and "our Father."

"If you then, being imperfect, know how to give good gifts to your children, how much more shall your Father who is in heaven give good things to those who ask him?" (Jesus in Matthew 7.11)

"Therefore, do not worry, saying, what shall we eat? or, what shall we drink? or, how shall get clothing? (Because all peoples seek after these things) Your heavenly Father knows that you have need of all these things." (Jesus in Matthew 6.31-32)

If God relates to us as a parent, and he is our creator, then our relationship to him should become that of a child who is loved by a good father. Peace and assurance should replace fear and guilt. God is no longer understood as a policeman waiting to pounce on lawbreakers. He is a father who wants his child to succeed and have an overflowing life. His love is more powerful than his need to punish.

Jesus told the parable of the Prodigal Son and shows us a father who is far more interested in who his son is becoming than in punishing him for his past mistakes. We understand the father to be God and we are the prodigals. God treats us like the father treated his wayward son. Wonderful!

This is great good news. And it changes how we view God and our relationship to him.

Jesus cared little for politics. He did not occupy himself with social issues. He paid little attention to the movements of nations. He was occupied with bringing new life to people. People seem to be the most important subject in his life.

Jesus' mission on Earth was all about the salvation of people, not society or nations. The value he placed on individual persons is strange for his times and place. His actions belie the value of each of us in the mind of God. Jesus valued nothing more than people.

"What do you think? If any man has a hundred sheep, and one of them is gone missing, does he not leave the ninety-nine, and go into the mountains, and search for the one that has gone astray? If he happens to find it, truly I say to you, he rejoices over it more than over the ninety-nine who have not gone astray." (Jesus in Matthew 18.12-13)

"I tell you, that even so there shall be joy in heaven over one off the mark person who changes his beliefs, more than over ninety-nine righteous persons who do not need to change." (Jesus in Luke 15.7)

The Old Testament story is about God's care for a chosen people, but also about the lives of individuals as they impact the condition of that race. The events are related to that race of people and the kind of lives they lived. God said that he would bless the world through them as a people.

The New Testament is all about persons and their individual lives. They are chosen people too, but as part of a spiritual kingdom rather than a physical one. Race and nationality are not issues at all. These "chosen" people shall also bless the world.

Jesus has shown us how much God cares for us

Jesus demonstrated by the way he related to persons the ways that God relates to us. He went about healing physical ailments and hurt spirits. He taught lessons about how to live to the fullest. He was obsessed with giving eternal life to everyone.

God has been so gracious to the world that he gave his only son ever to be born so that everyone who believes him may not be destroyed but may have eternal life. God did not send his son into the world to condemn the world, but so that the world might be saved through him. (John 3.16-17)

God has taken the initiative to see that his created children may become his spiritual offspring. He has not waited for us to find our way. He has taken the first step and brought life to us. He cares that much.

In a world that constantly tells people how unimportant they are, Jesus came to tell us how valuable we are to the Living God. The circumstances of life may beat the life out of us, but God is with us to see that we continue to have life, and have it full to overflowing. We are his delight.

The Father showers us with gifts

Jesus showed us that God showers us with blessings for living which we take for granted and usually do not recognize. We are like children who never understand the multitudes of care that their parents have heaped upon them.

The Parable of the Prodigal Son paints a story of a generous father who bequeaths a fortune to a son with little wisdom about how to use it. The story sounds far fetched because few fathers would ever be so generous to one who has not proven his judgment.

But, on reflection, Jesus was painting a picture of the Heavenly Father and the reality that he has bequeathed to each of us just such a fortune. He has given us years to live, talents to use, energy to expend, creativity to use, skills to display, and a multitude of other possessions. He has given each of us this kind of wealth without strings attached.

We may squander or misuse our treasure as we see fit. We may take our treasure of life and completely misuse it like the Prodigal did. We may use it up with little to show for it. Just as the father of the Prodigal gave him the freedom to expend his blessings, so God gives us the freedom to expend ours. That is gracious love of a kind which we have difficulty emulating.

Love must be great and wise to allow ones we love to be free to be who they are and who they want to be, even when we know they are making mistakes. Ordinary love protects, controls, and directs. Real love lets persons be free. God has allowed us to be free. But, he has never left us completely alone. He is always a prayer away waiting to guide, assist and strengthen as much as we will allow. The decision is ours.

Knowing that the Father cares and values us gives us the confidence to live life to the fullest and best. We know that he is there and that he loves us. That belief gives us power. It gives us life. If we do not believe it, the consequences are just as great.

4. God is a Happy God

If God is like Jesus, he is a God of happiness. Jesus constantly brought great joy to persons. Everyone whom he healed went away rejoicing. His teachings paint a kind of spirit and lifestyle that are positive and blessing.

To treat other people as well as we do ourselves is a recipe for happiness. To do to others as we would want done to ourselves is to guarantee that happiness results. The teachings of Jesus are filled with joy and happiness.

"I have spoken these things to you, so that my joy may be in you, and that your joy may be made full to overflowing." (Jesus in John 15:11)

What a picture! Jesus revealed and taught ways of understanding and living designed to fill persons to overflowing with joy. If the rich young ruler had been listening to him talk of these things, it is no wonder that he came seeking the life Jesus was promising, eternal life, life of the heavens, God's kind of life. He had everything the world could offer: youth, wealth, religiousness, and position. But he did not have the kind of life of which Jesus spoke. Overflowing joy had not been produced by all those things that he had. He did not have abundant life.

...according to the good news of the wonderfulness of the happy God, that was committed to my trust. (Paul in 1 Timothy 1:11)

193

Can you imagine the implications of this statement by Paul? Who knew that God is a happy God? No one, until Jesus showed us and taught us. The view of the world and the religions in it is one of angry gods. The gods of the world were gods of legalism, fear, and guilt. Paul had become the custodian of the truth about a happy God who gives joy to those who believe in him.

When one keeps this insight in mind and reviews the many teachings of Jesus, it becomes obvious that happiness and joy run through his instructions for living. Love, care, forgiveness, grace, and unselfishness are all concepts that embody joy and happiness, both for the giver and the receiver.

We usually paint Jesus as a super serious, otherworldly person devoid of laughter and joyousness. When we look more closely at what he did and what he taught, we find another picture being painted by the Scripture. We find persons who believed the message singing hymns in their prison cell. We find apostles who cannot stop talking about Jesus and his message. The message is so wonderful and happiness producing that they cannot stop telling everyone about it.

Look at the above verse in Timothy again. The message of happiness has been entrusted to Paul, and he understands the awesomeness of that trust. The world is in the dark about the joy of God. People do not know him as a happy God. Unless someone shares the revelation, the world will never know.

If persons will not believe that Jesus told the truth about a happy God, they will never be set free from the fearful lies of the Devil. The good news must be shared. It is too good to be kept under a bushel. Its light must be given to the world.

Nor is it any wonder that early Christians would die for their beliefs. If they recanted the wonderful good news that they knew to be true, how would anyone else ever know the truth? They must keep the message on target. They could not let it die. They would die first, just as Jesus did.

5. God is a Gifting God

The religious world at large is very aware that God visits destruction upon mankind. It assumes that tragedies in life are a sign that God is displeased with wrong-living people. Earthquakes, famines, disease, and recessions are God's reaction to the sinful actions of humans. Prophets, priests, and preachers have made a living by interpreting where the guilt should lie when disaster strikes.

Jesus showed us a different God. He showed us a God who is constantly blessing persons with good gifts, in spite of their bad behavior. Jesus did the same. He was not quick to punish sinners. He was more interested in helping sinners. He gave them gifts of his time, his patience, and his assistance. The Pharisees were quick to administer deserved punishment for violations of righteousness. Jesus was not.

"If you then, being imperfect, know how to give good gifts to your children, how much more shall your Father who is in heaven give good things to those who ask him?" (Jesus in Matthew 7.11)

Jesus taught his disciples to constantly give good gifts of behavior to persons who did not deserve them. A Samaritan would give assistance to a wounded man who in all likelihood despised Samaritans. Persons would return good for bad and never bad for bad. The persecuted would pray for their persecutors. These actions were good gifts to persons who had not earned them. They were acts of grace and *agape*. They were God's kind of acts.

Blessings often go unnoticed. Tragedy gets everyone's attention. Jesus revealed to us a God who is constantly blessing. He did not blame God for any tragedies. He showed him to be constantly giving blessings that were often overlooked. He showed us a happy God who delights in blessing people: saints and sinners alike.

"You have heard that it was said, 'You shall be gracious to your neighbor, and hate your enemy.' But I tell you, be gracious to your enemies, and pray for those who persecute you; so that you may be offspring of your Father who is in heaven: because he makes his sun to rise on the bad and the good, and sends rain on the just and the unjust." (Jesus in Matthew 5.43-45)

Satan is a murderer. He kills spirits, joys, dignity, peace, honor, and inner power. He is a liar who constantly implants falsehoods and misconceptions in the hearts and lives of everyone who lives. He paints pictures of God for us that are wrong and miss the mark. We suffer tragedy and immediately blame God. We go through hard times and wonder what we have done wrong to deserve such treatment from God. God is continually associated with the problems of our lives. And yet, all of these ideas are inaccurate to reality.

Jesus portrayed God as the source of all the good things that come our way. James said,

Every good gift and every fulfilling gift is from
above, and comes down from the Father of lights, in
whom there is no changing, nor shadow of turning.
(James 1.17)

This picture is strange to our ears and causes us
to rethink how we believe and understand. Instead of
being constantly reminded of our shortcomings and
mistakes when we think of God, Jesus said that we
should be looking for the multitude of gifts that a
Loving Father is constantly giving to us.

Instead of seeing God as a legalistic judge
constantly passing sentences, we should understand
that God is a caring father who loves to bless his
children in spite of their weaknesses and shortcomings.

The contemporaries of Jesus had great difficulty
with believing his revelations and opinions. They
were so different from that which everyone, including
the most religious, understood about the person and
actions of God. Could Jesus be right? The religious
lawyers and teachers around Jesus did not believe that
he was right in his understandings. They did not see
God as a gifting father. They knew him to be a
righteous and holy judge.

We would never have understood God to be as
Jesus showed him to be if he had not revealed him to
us in this way. We would have never been set free
from the lies of the Devil. We would still be enslaved
by understandings that miss the mark.

"You are from a diabolic father, and the
passions of your father you want to pursue. He was a

*killer from the beginning, and did not stand for truth,
because truth is not in him. Whenever he speaks
deceptively, he speaks from himself, because he is a
liar and the father of liars."* (Jesus in John 8.44)

Jesus said that he would tell us the truth and the
truth would set us free from understandings that are
disastrously untrue. Not just untrue, but also spirit-
and life-killing. After all, Satan is not just a liar. He is
a liar who uses his lies to kill. Understanding God in
ways that constantly heap guilt upon us is a false
understanding that robs us of peace and joy.

Believing Jesus changes everything. God is our
father who delights in pouring out blessings upon us.
And not just us, but everyone around us. He is in the
forgiving, redeeming, restoring, reconciling, and life-
giving business. Jesus showed us that the passion and
joy of God is in the blessing of people. Had it not
been for Jesus, we would never have known.

We have recently been introduced to a new
phrase in our language: "random acts of kindness".
These are actions promoted by Christian people to be
done in whatever situation a person may live and
move. They refer to any unexpected action that may
be a blessing to another person. As believers have
practiced this idea, they have discovered the wonderful
pleasure it brings to them and to those whom they
touch. The practice gives us insight into the spirit of
our gifting God. He gives gifts because it brings joy to
heaven. And it brings joy to those who believe and
follow.

So Jesus said to those Judeans who believed in him, "If you live by my teachings, you are truly my disciples. You shall know the truth, and the truth shall set you free." (John 8.31-32)

6. God Cares for All People

Amazingly, world religions and religious understandings of God are usually couched in racial, national, or geographic terms. Humans seem to naturally compete with those who are in some way different than they. There is a feeling of superiority instilled in each race and nation. In the world, it is always us versus them. Jews against Samaritans and Gentiles, Greeks against barbarians, Americans against the rest of the world. The mindset is universal and can be found among all peoples.

Within societies the same fondness for division exists. Classes exist. They may be educational, economic, geographic, religious or racial. Within single societies, religious differences separate people with each group thinking that they are more in tune with God than all the others. Differences are magnified by the people involved.

Jesus did not pay much attention to religious, racial, or nationalistic differences among people. He related graciously to everyone. Whether a Samaritan, Jew, Roman, or Gentile they were equally important to him. His closing commission to his disciples challenged them to overcome all such barriers.

Jesus came to them and spoke to them, saying, "All authority has been given to me in heaven and on earth. Therefore, go and make disciples of all peoples, immersing them in the name of the Father and of the Son and of the Holy Spirit: teaching them to observe all the things which I have instructed you. Lo, I am

with you always, even to the end of the age."
(Matthew 28.18-20)

We pay attention to racial, national, economic, societal, and religious labels. God does not. Our thinking needs to change.

When Jesus related to the persons in his life, he related to each the same. He looked into their hearts and spirits and sought to give them new life. Everyone needs life, and everyone is a candidate for life.

Be gracious to your neighbor

The second great commandment instructs persons to be gracious to their neighbors just as they are to themselves. When pressed by his listeners to better define who a neighbor might be, Jesus told the Parable of the Good Samaritan. He made a hero of a person who would never have been welcome into the neighborhoods of those listening.

Jesus did not define a neighborhood by race, class, religion, circumstance or distance. He simply said to be gracious to everyone, no matter who they might be. His inference was that God is concerned about everyone equally. Everyone is a product of his creation. They are all his physical sons and daughters, and he desires also for them to be his spiritual sons and daughters.

Peter struggled with equality before God

The New Testament records the struggle of Peter with his understanding that God sees everyone the same. Peter had difficulty in turning loose of the idea that the Jews were more special to God than all other peoples. He told the story of having a vision of a great sheet being lowered from heaven with all kinds of animals in it, those clean and those considered unfit for eating by the Jews. Through this vision God showed Peter that all races and nations were acceptable to him (Acts 10)

Peter was reprimanded by Paul in Antioch as he related the story to the Galatian Christians.

When Peter came to Antioch, I challenged him personally because he was at fault. Before some people came from James, he was eating with other races. But when they came, he drew back and separated himself from them because he was afraid of those of the Circumcision. (Galatians 2.11-12)

Later he would say,

Peter opened his mouth and said, "Truthfully, I am discovering that God does not think more highly of some persons than others. In every nation he who honors him, and lives righteously, is accepted by him." (Acts 10.34-35)

Today, religious people of all persuasions, Christian and non-Christian, have difficulty believing that God is working with all peoples in the world. We have the notion that God does not go where Christians do not go. That he does not move among other peoples of the world until a Christian comes to be among them. This idea portrays a very small image of the Living God of the universe. It places him in our small boxes of understanding. He is obviously God of the whole world and everyone in it. His presence is active everywhere and around everyone who lives.

We should assume that everyone has had some sort of spiritual inclination or nudging in their lives. We should assume that the Living God has been seeking a place in their hearts in the past. This assumption changes the way we think of others and changes the ways we relate to them.

When sharing our faith with someone else, it changes our attitude and approach if we think that God has already been working with the persons we approach. An opening question in a witnessing discussion could change to be, "How are you and God doing?" The question bears out our belief that God has already been dealing with the person with whom we are speaking, no matter who that person may be.

7. God is an Initiative-taking God

The world usually views its gods as much more reactive than active. It understands the actions of the gods to be in response to human rights and wrongs. Blessings are the gods' response to rights, and tragedies are the gods' response to wrongs. This belief explains the tragedies which befall humanity. Those tragedies are simply the actions of gods of retribution.

The Bible as a whole shows a different kind of God, and Jesus reveals him more completely. God is an initiative-taking God who is constantly acting to help people.

God inspired Abraham to leave his known world and go and begin a new race with new religious understandings about him.

God sent Moses to free his people from bondage in Egypt.

God sent prophets to constantly call people to right and give them his insight.

God sent Jesus to give us life in the midst of death.

God sent his Spirit to guide the lives of all who believe.

God inspired writers to record the story of Jesus and his teachings.

God continues to intrude in the hearts and lives of persons in need of freedom for spirit and life. His actions toward us are not simply reactions to our actions in life. They are edifying, redeeming, and blessing acts which never cease to come to us.

Humans are often in bondage and must be freed if they are to have life that is meaningful. The Hebrews were in the bondage of slavery in Egypt and God sent Moses to help them become free. Jesus revealed that persons are still in bondage, but it is a bondage of the mind and spirit. He said that he came to set persons free from this spiritual slavery.

So Jesus said to those Judeans who believed in him, "If you live by my teachings, you are truly my disciples. You shall know the truth, and the truth shall set you free." (John 8.31)

Jesus answered, "Truly, I say to you, everyone who practices error is a slave to error. A slave does not live in the house forever, but the son lives there forever. If then the son should set you free, you shall be truly free." (John 8.34-36)

Why do you not understand my message? Because you are unable to hear my teachings. You are from a destructive father, and the passions of your father you want to pursue. He was a killer from the beginning, and did not stand for truth, because truth is not in him. Whenever he speaks falsely, he speaks from himself, because he is a liar and the father of liars." (John 8.43-44)

The bondage addressed by Jesus is a bondage of the mind and understanding. People are controlled by their understandings and beliefs. If those beliefs are false and destructive, the lives of those persons are doomed to destruction. Jesus was sent by the Father to reveal the truth and set people free from the prison of the mind and spirit that dooms them here and hereafter.

Peter reminded us later that it is the will of God for everyone to experience this freedom of heart, mind and spirit.

The Lord is not neglecting his promise, as some understand negligence. He is exceedingly patient with you. He is not wishing that anyone should be destroyed, but that everyone might receive this change of belief and understanding. (2 Peter 3.9)

God continues to take the initiative toward his creation. He continues to extend the salvation which comes with the new life he has brought to us through Jesus. He does not wait for us to seek him. He is always moving to find us through the many initiatives he takes.

8. God is a God of Truth and Light

The spirit of this world is selfish, greedy, deceptive and deceitful. The spirit of God is exactly the opposite.

This is the message which we have heard from him and proclaim to you: God is light and there is no darkness in him at all. If we claim to have fellowship with him and live in the darkness, we lie and are not living the truth. If we live in the light as he is in the light, we have fellowship with each other, and the sacrifice of his son Jesus cleanses us from every missed mark. (1 John 1.5-7)

The world as a whole does not believe in living in the light. Honesty and truthfulness are seen as detriments to success and self-preservation. Deceit is a lifestyle that is necessary for personal, financial, and political success.

But, deceit also kills spirit, self respect, honor, and trust. As a lifestyle it misses the mark. It does not build life up. It tears life down. It is characteristic of persons who are spiritually dead but physically alive.

God does not practice deception and deceit. He is real and he operates out of reality, not fantasy. Deception creates fantasies about life and it's living. It erects beliefs that are not really true. It deceives most those who practice it.

Deceit and dishonesty instills fear and guilt in life. Persons know they are wrong when being untruthful, and they know there is the constant possibility that they will be found out. They may try to comfort themselves by thinking that everyone else is deceptive also, but the excuse seldom brings any relief for internal guilt.

Jesus was tempted to use deception to accomplish his mission on Earth. Just after his baptism, he was in the mountain alone and the devil tempted him to take advantage of the ignorance of his contemporaries.

The prevalent ideas about who the coming Messiah would be included that of him being invincible. The idea was based on an Old Testament psalm that was understood to be a messianic passage foretelling the coming Messiah.

Then the devil took him to the holy city, and he set him on the pinnacle of the temple, and said to him, "If you are the Son of God, throw yourself down, because it is written, 'He shall give his angels protection over you: and, with their hands they shall hold you up, so that you may not even strike your foot against a stone.'"[10] Jesus said to him, "It is also written, 'You shall not test the Lord your God.'" (Matthew 4.5-7)

Satan was providing Jesus with an out for sidestepping the physical suffering which he knew would come. He knew that he would be put to death, but the religious teachers of the day did not believe it to be so of the Messiah. Jesus could have deceptively

---

[10] Psalm 91.11-12.

taken advantage of their ignorance and misuse of Scripture and avoided the cross, but he did not. He refused to play games with the truth, even to prevent his coming suffering.

Jesus knew that the webs of deceit rob life of honor and joy. They burden life with fear and guilt. They destroy life. They cause life to miss the mark. They lead to ends that are not wanted by anyone. They lead to disaster.

The events of Jesus' life were living demonstrations of the personality of God. In a world that knew of deities like those in Roman mythology, who were just as deceptive as humans, Jesus was revealing a God who never walked in the darkness of deceit and deception. He is a God who is the truth and loves the truth.

"God is spirit, and they who worship him must serve him in spirit and truth." (Jesus in John 4.24)

9. God is a Life-giving God

    The characteristics above are those of the Living God. They define his spirit and actions. God is spirit and he moves in the world. And he wants to give new life to everyone who lives.

    God wants his spirit to live in everyone. He wants everyone to become like him in attitude, values, and lifestyle. He wants us to become holy as he is holy.

    Jesus began early to speak of this spirit and he was identified by John the Baptist as one who would bring the Spirit of God to everyone who believed.

    John bore witness saying, "I have seen the Spirit coming down as a dove out of heaven, and it dwelled in him. I did not know him, but the one who sent me to immerse in water, he said to me, 'Upon the one whom you see the Spirit descending and dwelling in him, it is he who immerses in the Spirit of God.'" (John 1.32-33)

    "Do not be perplexed that I said to you that it is necessary for you to be born from above. The wind blows where it chooses and you hear its sound, but do not know from where it comes and where it goes. The same is true of everyone who has been born of the Spirit." (Jesus in John 3.7-8)

    Paul wrote about this phenomenon of spiritual renewal and rebirth often. He painted a picture of us as houses for the Spirit of God.

Do you not know that you are the temple of God, and that the Spirit of God lives in you? (1 Corinthians 3.16)

What? Do you not know that your body is the temple of the Holy Spirit which is in you, which you have from God, and you are not your own? (1 Corinthians 6.19)

The presence of the Spirit of God in a life can be observed and appreciated. It gradually overcomes the old spirit of a person and creates a new one within. This new spirit expresses itself in values, attitudes and behavior that are like that of the Father and the Son. It embodies the teachings of Jesus about forgiveness, non-judgmentalism, graciousness, joy, kindness, and care as mentioned by Paul as the fruit of the Spirit. (Galatians 5.22-23)

The presence of the Spirit in persons creates new persons in old bodies. They become new creations in Christ. They begin to become the kinds of persons whom God has wanted from the time of creation. They become the kinds of persons humans were ordained to be from the beginning.

Therefore, if any man is in Christ, he is becoming a new creation. The old ways are passing away. Behold, they are becoming new. (2 Corinthians 5.17)

By his own will he brought us forth by means of the message of truth, so that we might be a kind of first editions of his creations. (James 1.18)

It is the desire of the Father that everyone living might have his Spirit in themselves, and experience the fullness of life which he has for them. That the living dead might be brought to life here and now. The message of Jesus is the means by which he causes these new creations to come into existence.

218

The Message of Jesus About
A Lifestyle That is an Overflow of a
Happy Heart

"Enter through the narrow gate. The gate is wide and the way is broad which leads to destruction, and there are many who enter through it. The gate is small and the way is narrow which leads to life, and there are few who find it." (Jesus in Matthew 7.13-14)

The secrets to successful living have always been mysteries. Great teachers have been holding forth on the subject throughout history. Psychologists and sociologists continue to study and discover the secrets of full life. Jesus said that he had the answers directly from God. He said that his teachings contain the secrets for life and living.

"It is the spirit that gives life. The physical produces nothing. The words that I speak to you, they are spirit, and they are life." (Jesus in John 6:63)

Below we compile a list of those ways of living that Jesus taught. They are behaviors that have powerful results in the lives of both the doer and those receiving such behavior. They all contribute to the abundant and overflowing life. They are the product of a spirit within a person that has been placed there by God himself. They illustrate the lifestyle of the eternal. They are the ways of God. They transform human life in absolutely marvelous ways.

Behavior is the natural expression of beliefs

I encourage you, brethren, through the kindnesses of God, to present your bodies a living sacrifice, holy, approved by God, which is your **spiritual worship**. *Do not be molded by the ways of this world.* **Be changed by the renewing of your thinking**, *so that you may demonstrate that which is the good and acceptable and whole will of God.* (Romans 12.1-2)

Persons behave in ways which express their beliefs; beliefs about God, life, themselves, and other people. Jesus constantly referred to the inner person and the hearts of persons when speaking about lifestyle. The ancients believed the heart to be the center of belief and thinking in persons. We connect the heart to emotions, they connected the stomach or bowels to emotions.

When Jesus and other New Testament writers referred to things being in the heart or from the heart, they were referring to what was in the minds of persons. They were addressing the problem of believing and thinking the wrong things. This issue is at the core of belief in Jesus. Belief in Jesus was never limited to his person only. It also included belief in his revelations and his teachings.

The teachings and revelations of Jesus present very different ways of thinking and believing. They present a different understanding of God than has ever been known. They challenge ordinary ways of thinking about other people. They challenge value systems and life perceptions. They call for a different way of believing about most important things in life.

"A good man expresses that which is good out of the good treasure of his heart; and an evil man expresses that which is evil out of the evil treasure of his heart: because the mouth speaks out of an overflow of the heart." (Luke 6.45)

The message of Jesus, when understood and believed, changes the spirit, lifestyle, and value system of believers. They become different from the inside out. Their beliefs change and therefore their lives change.

Belief in grace can change everything. Legalism is the way of the world. It is the "way the world turns." People believe that persons should get what they deserve. That justice demands that persons be rewarded according to their just desserts. Therefore, constant assessments must be made and verdicts handed out. People simply treat other people as they think they deserve to be treated.

Grace changes everything. Belief in grace instructs us to treat persons well even if it is undeserved. The belief issues forth in behavior that is not legalistic. It brings forth behavior that is a gift to others. That gift may be forgiveness, help, prayer, peace, or any other desirable behavior that may be given from a "heart" of grace.

The Second Great Commandment laid the basis for our understanding and behavior toward other people.

"A second [commandment] like it is this, you shall be gracious to [agapao] your neighbor as you are to yourself." (Jesus in Matthew 22.39)

To believe in grace and to behave with graciousness results in a lifestyle that demonstrates grace to everyone around us. But the behavior will not happen unless belief precedes it. If we do not believe in grace, we will not practice graciousness.

The Christian lifestyle is built on the foundation of grace. The many behaviors, like forgiveness, are the natural result of a happy heart and belief in the grace shown to us by Jesus.

Persons come to a new life when they change their thinking and begin to think like the Son and the Father. They become persons of joy, grace, and *agape*.

Behavior either builds up or tears down

Some behaviors may be neutral in their affects on self and others, but most are not. Actions either produce help to life or they take away from life. Behavior has a consequence for the inner person as well as to other people around about. They help or they hurt. They give life or they diminish life.

Jesus taught a lifestyle that fills up the inner person as well as it blesses others. It is a lifestyle that is filled with joy. It is dignified and honorable. It gives rather than takes. It creates rather than destroys. It is the life that he called abundant or overflowing.

"I have come so that you may have life, and have it to the overflow." (Jesus in John 10.10)

How to be gracious to a neighbor

The basis for the lifestyle taught by Jesus is the second Great Commandment, but he did not stop with that general instruction. He was constantly giving examples of how to be gracious to neighbors, many of them hostile. Jesus sprinkled his many teachings with ways to be a person of grace and happiness in our world.

The following behaviors are expressions of being a joyous person of grace and *agape*. They are the natural outgrowth of the happy, gracious spirit of God in a life. Although separate in our descriptions, they are all intertwined. They are individual facets of one diamond, the diamond of joy and grace. Each behavior looks at the diamond from a different perspective, yet all look at the same diamond.

Each of these behaviors contribute to all the others. They are an interrelated family of "good deeds." None is exclusive of the others. All are part of the same whole.

There is value at looking at each separately because each represents a specific lifestyle activity. Each shows a specific understanding and mindset which helps clarify the whole. Jesus and his apostles spoke to each in their teachings and revelations.

The following ways of living are not natural and normal for persons. They are ways that come from the special truth, wisdom and understandings brought to us by Jesus. Some will say that they are unrealistic and unworkable. Some will not. The key is belief. If one is willing to believe in Jesus and believe in his teachings, then believing in each of these ways of living is more natural. But, they have to be believed for them to be effective in life. Unbelief prevents the practice of each, and therefore, prevents the life-filling results of that belief and practice.

"He who is not gracious to me, does not observe my teachings, and the teachings which you hear are not mine, but are from the Father who sent me."
(Jesus in John 14.24)

Happiness is a characteristic of the Jesus life

The teachings of Jesus and the New Testament are filled with references to joy and happiness. Strangely, the word for happiness has been universally translated into English as "blessed". Greek scholars are well aware that the word *makarioi* means happiness or to be happy. Yet, they continue to insist that it be translated as "blessed", which conveys an altogether different meaning. Some Christian theology is so negative and guilt-ridden that it cannot bring itself to think of God as being a happy God. Nor does it see him in the business of helping persons experience lives of happiness. But, Jesus said the opposite.

He said, "To the contrary, happy are they who hear the message of God, and practice it." (Jesus in Luke 11.28)

"Since you know these things, you are happy if you practice them." (Jesus in John 13.17)

When one begins to understand that the Good News is all about happiness and joy, the concept can be detected throughout the New Testament. Happiness and joy are sprinkled all through the chapters. The first disciples experienced this new experience of God and could not wait to share it with all those around them who worshipped angry gods. It was radically good news to all who heard it and believed in Jesus and his message.

The many lifestyle instructions of Jesus are far more doable if we understand that they are preceded by a happy heart. Happy people do things the unhappy never attempt.

People with a happy spirit forgive more quickly.

People with a happy spirit go second miles more pleasantly.

People with a happy spirit are more prone to return good for bad.

People with a happy spirit pray for their persecutors.

People with a happy spirit see no need to be judgmental.

People with a happy spirit find it easier to care for the poor and needy.

People with a happy spirit gift other people like they would like to be gifted far faster.

The Spirit of God is a spirit of happiness, joy, and grace and that spirit issues forth in the kind of behavior we explore below. Jesus was happy and he instructed us how to live lives that are overflows of a happy heart.

Caution! Be Wise and Not Naive

We begin with a caution. These behaviors will seem very unreasonable and undoable. They will sound naïve and Pollyanna. Yet, Jesus taught that we should live them. He gave us very little wiggle room to ignore them. But he did give us a couple of caveats.

"Look out! I am sending you out as sheep surrounded by wolves, so be as smart as snakes and as innocent as doves." (Jesus in Matthew 10.16)

This is a powerful and insightful injunction. Using animal personalities like sheep, wolves, snakes and doves speaks volumes about his honest evaluation of people in the world. He was saying, "Let's be real with our living." We cannot pretend that people are different than they really are. Wolves are not passive creatures. They are predators. We should learn to recognize them when we encounter them.

To be smart as snakes may not be very easy for most people. But it does paint a picture of persons who do not forego their common sense as they pursue the ideals that Jesus taught.

"Do not give that which is holy to dogs, nor put your pearls on pigs, because they will trample them under their feet, and turn around and attack you." (Jesus in Matthew 7.6)

Disciples are to be realistic enough to know when to be gracious and when it is a waste of care and effort. Giving gifts of care or help to some people is a predictable waste of time. It will accomplish nothing, nor will it change anyone for the good. Be realistic. Do not waste time and effort. The gift of prayer may be the only effective gift extended to such persons.

Becoming proficient at knowing "when to hold them and when to fold them" may require some years of experience. Those years of experience may include suffering through some very disappointing and hurtful times.

A life of grace is not simple in application. One must learn its "ins and outs." But, let us not be foolish and naïve. Let us be real, but be who we want to be personally, regardless of the world around us.

1. Walking with the Living God is the Way of Joy and Peace

"Live in me, and I in you. For the branch is not able to bear fruit from itself, it must be connected to the vine. Neither can you unless you live in me. I am the vine, you are the branches. He who lives in me, and I in him, will bear much fruit. Because separated from me, you cannot accomplish anything." (Jesus in John 15.4-5)

Biblical history is filled with the experiences of men and women who daily walked with God. They were aware of the presence of God in their lives, and his care for who they were in their lives. They were distinguished by their humble commitment to do the will of God as they understood his leadership.

The cares and pressures of living often crowd out our sensitivity to the presence of God in and around us. On occasion, we decide that we will not prosper if we limit our behavior to that which is pleasing to God, and we choose other behaviors. We have many reasons to live as though God does not. When we do so, we lose life.

We need the daily help and guidance of the presence of God to be able to experience the life that only he can give to us. He leads us to life through the teachings of Jesus and through the inner nudging of his Spirit in us.

If we attempt to "go it alone" we miss the mark too often and wind up where we did not intend to be.

We need the constant help of the Father. And we need the humility that is expressed in our desire to allow the Father to be our guide and help.

The lie

The spirit of this world leads us to believe that we do not need God to live our lives well. We do not need his instructions about how to live to have a full life.

That lie is compounded by our ideas that the prohibitions of God take the joy out of life. We do not like to be curtailed in our passions and desires. We ignorantly think that life can be more full with an "anything goes" philosophy.

We never learn. Life history is filled with examples that can give us insight into the disastrous results of unbridled living. We simply do not want to know. We have been brainwashed by lies that feed our misplaced ego and pride. And, we pay the price and it is dear.

Jesus said above that we need our connection to him if we are to see life results that we dream of having. We simply have to believe that to be true and walk daily with sensitivity to his presence and ways. Less humility means less fullness.

He hath shewed thee, O man, what is good; and what doth the Lord require of thee, but to do justly, and to love mercy, and to walk humbly with thy God? (Micah 6.8 KJV)

2. A Spirit of Joy is Gracious

"And a second [commandment] like it is this, you shall be gracious to [agape] your neighbor as you are to yourself." (Jesus in Matthew 22.39)

"You have heard that it has been said, you shall be gracious to your neighbor, and hate your enemy. But I say unto you, be gracious to your enemies, bless those who curse you, do good to those who hate you, and pray for those who despitefully treat you and persecute you; so that you may be the offspring of your Father who is in heaven: for he makes his sun to rise on the evil and on the good, and sends rain on the just and on the unjust." (Jesus in Matthew 5:38-45)

"If you are gracious to those who are gracious to you, what joy is in that? Don't the tax collectors do the same thing? If you show respect to your brethren only, what makes you different from anyone else? Don't the tax collectors do the same thing?" (Jesus in Matthew 5.46-47)

"Do not be judgmental unless you want to be judged by others. The way you judge others will be the way they judge you, and the standards you use will be used on you." (Jesus in Matthew 7.1-2)

We have dealt extensively with grace and *agape* above, but it is important to repeat that this approach to living is a bedrock basis for the Jesus lifestyle. Grace is the foundation for understanding the various life teachings of Jesus. They all demonstrate ways to be gracious to other people and to God.

Treat people better than they deserve

Legalism says treat people as they deserve. Grace teaches us to treat people far better than they deserve. Our treatment is a gift not a reward. We behave like the Father and the Son regardless of what people deserve. We are not motivated by justice. We are motivated by the ways of God.

We recognized that life can become a vicious and deadly cycle of getting even if we only relate to people with just dessert ways. We want peace and we want joy. We are world changers not simply people who perpetuate the problems that already exist.

Treat people with gifting joy

The meaning of grace is to be gifting to others and to bring joy to them. We give happy gifts to people in our lives. After all, that is the goal of everyone, that is, to experience joy and happiness. When we contribute to that happiness, we are helping persons experience that which they desire most.

That is being people of grace and *agape*. That is doing the work of God. It is the doing of the "good deeds" mentioned in the King James Version. It is world-changing and life-changing.

Treating people as they deserve without an attempt to help them experience joy is the same old way of the world. It changes nothing. We are no different than anyone else. When we do grace to persons, we are different people than the world knows. It causes us to become different and our world becomes different.

We become new creations like Christ. We begin to behave like the Father and the Son. We begin to have the same life in us that they have in themselves. We begin to be persons who overflow with grace.

If you are gracious to those who are gracious to you, have you really done anything? Do not even the hated tax collectors do that? If you only speak to your brothers, what makes you different from anyone else? Do not even the hated tax collectors do so? (Jesus in Matthew 5.46-47)

3. A Spirit of Joy Loves Truth, Honesty, and Integrity

"A time is coming and is now, when true worshippers will serve the Father in spirit and truth, because the Father desires such persons to serve him. God is spirit, and they who worship him must serve him in spirit and truth." (Jesus in John 4.23-24)

Jesus said to those Judeans who were believing in him, "If you live by my teachings, you are truly my disciples. And you shall know the truth, and the truth shall set you free." (John 8.31-32)

Truth emphasizes reality not fantasy.

The world is filled with deceit and deception. Persons have felt no hesitation to lie their way out of bad situations. Business people consider it part of good business to paint the most appealing picture of their products, whether accurate or not. Politicians do not hesitate to put as much "spin" as necessary on subjects they promote. Crusaders do not mind being deceptive about their causes, and refer to their deceptions as being "partisan." Partisan sounds so much better than deceit.

Deception and deceit can become a way of life.

Dishonesty has not changed since the times of Jesus. His world was just as deceitful as ours, perhaps more so. The Jewish world was filled with merchants and traders. Many of these were astute at deceiving their customers and clients. Deception was an accepted way of life. It is no wonder that the New Testament thought it important to record the first encounter of Jesus with Nathaniel:

Jesus saw Nathaniel coming toward him, and said about him, "Look, an Israelite indeed, in whom there is no deceit!" (John 1.47)

Evidently, this was a significant statement to say about a person of the day. Deception was everywhere and must have been the accepted norm for living. That made Nathaniel an unusual person.

Jesus taught a different lifestyle. Deceit has a price that has nothing to do with money. It robs persons of self-respect, honor, and inner peace. It disrespects others and does not mind taking advantage of them. It poisons relationships and the persons involved. It robs life of life. Deceit makes life less than it can be. It stifles the overflow.

Now, this is the communication that we have heard from him and share with you: God is light and there is absolutely no darkness in him. If we say that we are one with him, and we behave in dark ways, we are being deceptive. We are not being truthful. But, if we will walk in the light, like he is in the light, we have fellowship with one another, and the blood of his son Jesus Christ frees us from missing the mark. (1 John 1.5-7)

4. A Spirit of Joy is Active Rather than Reactive

"I say to you, be gracious to your enemies, bless those who curse you, do good to those who hate you, and pray for those who despitefully treat you and persecute you; so that you may be the offspring of your Father who is in heaven." (Jesus in Matthew 5.39f)

The motivation for much of our behavior results from the previous behavior of other persons. We treat other people as reactions to the ways in which they have treated us.

This way of living is so natural to our thinking that it is almost automatic or "knee jerk" in our lives. We simply respond in natural ways to the treatment or circumstances of living.

Regrettably, we practice "do unto others as they have done unto you" far better than "do unto others as you would have them do unto you." We return the good expressed to us, but not nearly so well as the bad that comes our way. We are simply creatures of reactive responses.

Jesus taught a more controlled lifestyle. He disdained automatic responses in kind. He taught that we should be in control of our behavior, with the help of the Spirit, to the extent that we can deliberately decide how we respond to the behavior of others toward us.

Become a force for good

In addition, Jesus taught principles that direct us to be active toward others in positive ways.

And a second [commandment] like it is this, you shall be gracious to [agape] your neighbor as you are to yourself. (Matthew 22.39)

The very idea that we would treat the people around us as well as we treat ourselves goes against our natural and normal understandings. We are much more at home with Cain's response "Am I my brother's keeper?" We normally look out for me and mine and expect everyone else to do the same for they and theirs.

Treat others as you want to be treated. (Luke 6.31)

This teaching illustrates the proactive aspect of the Jesus Way. Rather than reacting to the behavior of others, Jesus taught that we should take the initiative in relationships, and be as positive and helpful as we want others to be toward us. This is the first half of a concept that emphasizes the affects we can expect from our actions toward others. This is the positive aspect. But there is also a negative side to it.

Do not be judgmental unless you want to be judged by others. The way you condemn others will be

the way they condemn you, and the standards you use
will be used on you. (Matthew 7.1-2)

Just as we can expect our positive behavior to
respond in kind, so we can expect our negative actions
to bring negative responses. This is the same idea
contained n the popular saying, "what goes around,
comes around." This insight is powerful for those who
make it their tool rather than their master. We can
have great influence over the affects of our behavior
toward others if we pay attention and act accordingly.
That is, if we choose to *overcome bad with good.*

With this kind of lifestyle we take charge of our
behavior and make our living a force for good in our
world. It challenges us to be an aggressive blessing to
the people in our lives. It changes our spirit and
motivation and puts us on the offensive rather than the
defensive. Over time, we become accomplished at
knowing how to bless people with our living.

Refusing to be reactive is amazing!!

Break the spiral of bad

When we react to the negative actions of others
with the same kind of behavior as they, we create a
cycle of destructive living. Usually this leads to an
upward spiral of worse and worse behavior as we try
to outdo each other with worse and worse punishment.
This is the material of feuds and wars. Jesus taught us
to break this cycle by refusing to react in kind.

"I say to you, be gracious to your enemies, bless those who curse you, do good to those who hate you, and pray for those who despitefully use you and abuse you." (Matthew 5.44)

This kind of behavior is not as far-fetched as it may seem at first glance. It simply instructs us to take charge of our lives and control our behavior toward others in spite of what they may do toward us.

It also alerts us to the truth that continued hurtful actions never get the desired results. They simply motivate our enemies to try harder to destroy us and ours. They never make relationships better nor resolve the issues involved.

Be wise and realistic

Being gracious does not mean to be "patsies." Jesus was no Casper Milquetoast. He did not allow persons to abuse him, not until it came time for the cross. He spoke the truth and stood his ground. At the same time, he was gracious in that he did not retaliate and seek to punish his attackers. He resisted attack, but did not attack back.

Jesus, as usual, instructs us to take the initiative in making our relationships and our world in our image rather than allow others to control us. Paul expanded on this later in his letter to the Romans.

Do not be overpowered by the bad, but overpower bad with good. (Romans 12.21)

This injunction may seem impossible at first but it can be done with some success. When attempted regularly, one can experience victory every so often. The key to the teaching is that we should attempt this as a lifestyle, and as we do so it changes our thinking and behavior.

5. A Spirit of Joy Forgives People

Peter came to him and said, "Lord, how often shall my brother wrong me, and I forgive him? As many as seven times?" Jesus said to him, "I do not tell you as many as seven times: but, as many as seventy times seven." (Matthew 18.21-22)

Forgiveness gets a bad rap from most people. They consider the idea to be naïve and weak. But the kind of forgiveness that Jesus taught was any thing but.

To forgive in the New Testament means to not respond to others in the manner they deserve. It means to forego the negative treatment of others that they have earned from us.

Once again, forgiveness is the opposite of the normal reaction to the actions of others. It actually teaches us not to be controlled in our behavior by that which has been done to us.

The opposite of forgiveness is revenge or repayment

Revenge is treating others like they have treated us. It is allowing them to determine our relationship. If our behavior is simply a reaction to theirs, they are in charge of the relationship. We are not. We simply react in predictably negative ways.

To forgive allows us to refuse to treat persons in the negative ways in which they deserve to be treated. Rather, we act as we choose and as God wants us to act. We are not allowing the negative actions of others to dictate our lifestyle. When we forgive, we let what another has done go past us as though it did not happen. It did happen, and we know it, but we choose not to respond as though it happened. We respond in our own ways, as we choose.

Jesus said to forgive "seventy times seven" to illustrate that this way of relating to people should become a lifestyle, not a rare event. We are to cultivate the habit of never repaying the hurts of others, but instead to bless them in some way. We must take better charge of our lives, and respond in more beneficial ways. Refusing to pay back in kind becomes a lifestyle choice. And it is a Jesus lifestyle choice.

Do not be naïve

Jesus did not teach that we should just roll over in the face of mistreatment by others. He put some caveats in place to let us know that we are not to behave weakly or foolishly. Without these cautions, forgiving can cause us to become an abused doormat for persons who love to take advantage of the weak.

Recall what we said on this subject in the section entitled "Caution: Don't be Naïve." We are to be wise in our ways of grace, not foolish. Forgiveness is a powerful tool in our living for the Father, but we are not to be stupid in our use of it.

Forgiveness is a two way street

Forgiveness is obviously a blessing to those in our debt whom we forgive for what they may have done to us. It frees them from the normal results of their wrong actions. It is one of the ways in which we bless our neighbors and do to others as we would want for ourselves. But forgiveness is not a one-way street. It also blesses the one doing the forgiving.

Forgiveness is the means by which the hurts of the past are cast out of our lives. When we harbor the hurts that have been done to us by others, those hurts grow in their ability to steal our joy. The hurt continues to plague us. When we forgive a guilty person, it breaks the power of past hurt in our lives. It cuts off the influence of that hurt in our minds and emotions. It sets us free from the past so that we can concentrate on our hopes for tomorrow. Forgiveness actually does more for the one doing the forgiving than it does for the one being forgiven. It is a life-giving and joy-creating lifestyle.

6. A Spirit of Joy Overcomes Bad with Good

"I say to you, be gracious to your enemies, bless those who curse you, do good to those who hate you, and pray for those who despitefully use you and persecute you." (Matthew 5.44)

Do not be overpowered by the bad, but overpower bad with good. (Romans 12.21)

Each of the lifestyle ways contribute to this overcoming. The hoped for results of each way is the presence of more peace and joy in the lives involved. When we practice the ways of Jesus we are practicing ways to overcome the bad in life. We are contributing to good in life. They produce good and overcome bad. They produce a measure of peace and happiness instead of antagonism and suspicion.

Jesus did not leave us without means for accomplishing his instructions. He taught and demonstrated in his own life the ways to change ourselves and the world around us, for the good.

Jesus showed us the ways to defuse the bad and promote good. His teachings were often about how to act in hostile situations. He taught us how to change those events into less hostility.

We are empowered in this mission by the knowledge that Jesus and the Father live this kind of lifestyle. When we practice the ways of Jesus, we are practicing the ways of God. We are being his people in a world that does not know how to live in peace and joy.

7. A Spirit of Joy is a Spirit of Peace

"Happy are the peacemakers, because they shall be called the sons of God." (Jesus in Matthew 5:9)

"...leave your offering at the alter and go and make peace with your brother or sister, and then come and offer your gift." (Jesus in Matthew 5:24)

If it is possible, as much as it is in your power, be at peace with everyone. (Romans 12.18)

So then, let us do those things which make for peace, and things by which we may edify one another. (Romans 14.19)

Let the peace of Christ rule in your hearts, to which also you were called into one body; and be thankful. (Colossians 3.15)

Personal peace is one of life's great treasures.

Religion often attempts to fill our lives with guilt, fear, and dread. When it does so, personal peace disappears if it ever existed in the first place. A religious emphasis on laws and lawbreakers is a sure destroyer of any peace that we might come to know. A belief that God is going to punish us for what we do wrong makes peace flee from our hearts and lives. It puts us at odds with God. We become estranged and fearful.

Jesus revealed that we misunderstand God when we believe that he is in the judgment and punishing business. Believing such about him robs us of life. He did not minimize the reality of sin. It is a powerful, destructive force in the lives of everyone. He simply revealed that God is not the one handing out the destructive results of sin. That is not his spirit.

Jesus said that God is a God of peace. He wants peace with us and he wants us to be at peace with ourselves and those around us. When we experience and pursue peace in our lives, we are behaving like the Father. We are being like children of the Heavenly Father.

Paul clarified that God is a person of peace

Paul experienced a personal transformation from being a person of anger and hatred to becoming a person of peace. When he began to believe in the message and revelations of Jesus, he began to have peace in his spirit and soul. He stopped fighting against the "goad" and he let the peace of God come into him.

Later, Paul wrote to the Galatian Christians about the true spirit of God. He was speaking against their desire to serve a god of legalism and defined the true spirit of the Father.

Paul began his list of characteristics of God with "graciousness, joy, peace…". When the spirit of God comes into the life of a believer, this is the kind of person it creates. This is who God is and this is the effect of his presence in a life. His is a spirit of peace

When we begin to be submissive to the will of God, we begin to become people with a spirit of peace in our hearts and lives. In addition, we begin to become people who desire to make peace among everyone.

Peace and peacefulness sets life free and allows it to become its best. Peaceful people are blessings to everyone. They are people who are truly alive.

The Father wants us to be at peace and to make peace with the persons in our world.

The techniques for making peace are depicted in many of the other lifestyle teachings of Jesus. Refusing to react in kind, forgiving those who do not deserve it, and being a person of grace are all means for making peace. As additional lifestyle ways are discussed below it will become obvious that they can be builders of peace also. The lifestyle of Jesus is a lifestyle of peace and peacemaking.

Peace is an absence of fear

Life is filled with fears. We are afraid of possible future hurts and harms. We are afraid of failure. We are afraid of disease and sickness. We are afraid of dying. We are people who know fears of all kinds.

John said that *agape* pushes out fear.

There is no fear in graciousness. Full grown graciousness pushes fear out. Fear is punishment. He who fears has not become complete in graciousness. (1 John 4.18)

The teachings of Jesus about the love of God for us paint a picture of a Heavenly Father who cares and constantly blesses us. He guards our lives and our futures. He is not in the zapping business. He is compassionate toward us and our living. He walks with us through our valleys of life and gives us direction and encouragement. He lives toward us these various ways that Jesus teaches us to be toward others. He is a God of peace who is creating a people of peace. What a blessed idea!

8. A Spirit of Joy Builds other People Up

Jesus is the great physician who came to heal those in need. He touched lives with a positive and healing touch. No matter how sinful the person, Jesus touched the life with positive power. Even his relationship to the authorities, money changers, and Pharisees was intended to result in positive change. Jesus was in the life-changing business, and the changes he wrought were wonderfully positive and edifying.

Jesus had a healing touch

Jesus never destroyed life, character, or reputation. He built up each life he touched. He healed, transformed, and inspired those with whom he came into contact.

Paul reminded his readers in later writings,

So then, let us do those things that make for peace, and things by which we may edify one another. (Romans 14.19)

All things may be lawful, but all things are not expedient. All things may be lawful, but all things do not edify. Let no one be concerned only about his own, but also his neighbor's good. (1 Corinthians 10.23-24)

Edification is the answer to the reply of Cain when he said, "Am I my brother's keeper?" The answer is a resounding, "Yes!" We are to be concerned about how our actions impact those around us. It is not enough to deliberately choose not to destroy the lives, reputations, peace, and joy of other people. We must seek to contribute to the lives of our neighbors.

The original Commandment not to bear false witness is a part of this concern. When we are dishonest in our reports about someone else, we are destroying them one word at a time. The Jesus Way is to always be constructive rather than destructive to persons, their reputations, peace and joy. Can we always succeed at this? Not hardly, but it is our goal and desire.

Edifying in spite of wrong

Do we simply ignore the wrongs in life and in people as though they do not exist? Absolutely not. We are also people of truth and reality. We are to be constructive in spite of the wrong involved. We are to be realistic about the circumstances of our living, but not be controlled by the wrongs we face. Being *as smart as snakes and as harmless as doves* is a passion that takes every skill we have to accomplish. Our success at overcoming with edification is that we are about the business of our Father, and he is involved with us. This is his lifestyle as well as ours. We are not alone in this enterprise. He is moving behind the scenes to bless what we do. We simply do and trust the outcomes to him.

9. A Spirit of Joy is Humble

"Happy are the humble, because they shall inherit the Earth." (Matthew 5.5)

"When you receive an invitation, go and take a seat at the lowliest place, so that when he who invited you comes, he may say to you, 'Friend, go up to a more prestigious place.' Then you will have appreciation in the eyes of those who are eating with you." (Luke 14.10)

"Take my yoke upon you, and learn from me, because I am gentle and humble in heart, and you shall find rest for your souls." (Matthew 11.29)

When pride comes, shame comes. But with the humble is wisdom. (Proverbs 11.2)

Humility is not passive

Humility is different than competitive aggressiveness. The world usually thinks that the most competitive and aggressive people will get the most from life. This teaching of Jesus calls that idea into question.

The picture being painted by these teachings of Jesus is of a person who may be aggressive and may be competitive but at the same time practice these Jesus ways. One may be a "go getter" and still not trample on other people while being so.

Humility defines the heart of a person who has as much respect for others as he does for himself.

One may be competitive without being prideful. One may be competitive without being ruthless. One may be aggressive without being cutthroat.

Bill Glass was an all pro defensive tackle for the Chicago Bears football team. In his career, he was only whistled for a personal foul one time. Following the call, he immediately apologized to the umpire and the player involved making sure that they understood that he would never deliberately hurt another person. He was competitive enough to be an all pro, but not at the cost of dirty or dishonest play. Bill was aggressive but humble.

God gifts the humble

An interesting part of this teaching is the inheritance idea in Matthew 5.5. An inheritance is a gift, usually an unearned gift. It is normally given by a parent to a child, and in this case from the Heavenly Father to his children. Jesus is reminding us that most of what we have is a gift from God to start with. We have life that is a gift from God. We have talent that is gift from God. We have abilities that are a gift from God. We have our days on this Earth that are a gift from God.

None of these things came about because of our aggressive and competitive abilities and efforts. We have inherited them from our Heavenly Father. We should, therefore, be humble in the face of so many unearned gifts. We are no different than everyone else in that we have gifts beyond what we have earned for ourselves. To use the abilities God has given us to take advantage of others whose gifts are not as powerful as ours is to disregard the one who has given gifts to all.

God does not play favorites

The Father does not love us more than he loves others. This is a hard and difficult truth. We prefer to think otherwise. But when he instructs us to be as gracious to others as we are to ourselves, he states that reality rather clearly. He expects us to be humble people who love to bless and edify others as well as ourselves.

This teaching takes the hard-nosed competitiveness out of our lives. We are to be more responsible for our brothers and sisters. We are not to elevate ourselves and ours above all others. We are to be people of humility.

Is it possible to be humble and competitive at the same time? Yes! Competitiveness often brings out the best of our abilities. It challenges us to improve, focus, be motivated, and achieve. Competitiveness is not automatically evil. But, the way one goes about being competitive may be evil. When the goal becomes more important than people, that becomes problematic. We are to be gracious to those with whom we compete. That is the Christian difference.

10. A Spirit of Joy Blesses People with More than is Required

In the Sermon on the Mount, Jesus said to,

Go one more mile than required.
Give more in court than is required. (Matthew 5.40-41)
Bless when it is not expected.
Be generous to those who cannot repay.
Forgive when it is not expected.

More is magic! More changes everything. More blesses the one giving more and the one receiving more.

Jesus taught the kind of lifestyle that is not satisfied to only do the required and expected. There is little satisfaction in only doing the expected. He noted that anyone can do that. His audience hated tax collectors and referred to them as being sinners, but Jesus said:

"If you are gracious to those who are gracious to you, what joy is in that? Don't the tax collectors do the same thing? If you show respect to your brethren only, what makes you different from anyone else? Don't the tax collectors do the same thing?" (Matthew 5.46-47)

Be different, do more

God expects Christians to be wonderfully different than everyone else. Not just different, but wonderfully different. We are to inject goodness into their world. We are not to settle for the ordinary in life. We are taught to bless our world with gifts of grace.

What an adventure! To think that God wants us to be a surprise to the world. Not just any surprise, but a happy surprise.

Joe Greene, founder of Health Management Associates, believes in doing more than is expected. He and his brother instituted a policy at the company that required all company bills to be paid by return mail, even those not due for sixty days. No one expected to be paid so quickly, nor did they require it. Joe is different. He does more than is expected or required. Many clients have called to ask why he follows a practice that is not required, but is appreciated. He is happy to tell them that as a Christian he enjoys doing more.

A "baker's dozen" has been known for generations. Bakers have routinely given thirteen items when twelve have been ordered. The extra is a gift. It is more than has been paid for. Obviously, the practice is designed to produce goodwill and appreciation for the baker. It gives joy to the customer, and that in turn, gives joy to the baker. Doing more creates joy in life.

Doing more is a happy task

The British preacher, Charles Spurgeon, said that Christians were the only people in the ancient world who served a happy God. We should be able to say that about the Christians of any age, because that is God's intent. Jesus showed us a Father who is delightfully caring and helping. He forgives, reconciles, supports and blesses. He is a joyous God who loves to do joyous things for mankind. We are to be like him.

If you, being imperfect, love to give good gifts to your children, how much more will your Father who is in heaven give good gifts to those who ask him? (Matthew 7.11)

More matters

The result of going one mile as required by the law normally leaves the parties involved fuming at each other when the mile is completed. Going the second mile, which is not required, changes things. An undeserved gift is given to the person who insists on getting what the law enforces. The second mile is not forced and cannot be forced. It is freely given by the one being coerced. The end result is different. Both parties view the experience differently than if only one mile were traveled. One has received a free gift, the other has the joy of giving a gift. The outcome is drastically different than before.

The court case is a similar example. A person is guilty of some illegal action and is required by the court to pay up. The person receiving the payment knows it is deserved and feels justified in his animosity toward the guilty party. When more is given than the court required, the emotions of the situation change. It is difficult to harbor spiteful feelings toward someone who has given more than required. More changes things. More is magic.

Serve a happy God

Simply meeting the expectations of life is an accomplishment, but going beyond expectations is a *joyful* accomplishment. It adds a dimension of wonder and goodness to life and living. What a wonderful way to live! It is no wonder that the teachings and life of Jesus were called the "good message" or "good news." Everything about him and his teachings and lifestyle were good and joyous and happy.

11. A Spirit of Joy is Guided by the Prompting of the Spirit Within

"I will request from the Father that he give you another Guide, and he will give you one that will remain with you forever, the spirit of truth, whom the world cannot accept because it does not recognize it nor understand it. But you understand it because it lives in you, and shall be in you." (Jesus in John 14.16-17)

"The things which I have said to you are living in you. 26. The Guide, the spirit of God, which the Father will send, consistent with me, will teach you everything, and will help you remember everything which I said to you." (Jesus in John 14.25-26)

The spirit of God is a flowing force in the world. Jesus said it is like the wind. It blows and touches lives, and its results and influence can be seen. It is both taught and caught.

The presence of God is all around everyone

The spirit of God is working in the world in the lives of everyone. No one whom we meet will have escaped the inner voice of God speaking to his heart. Peter made the point that God does not want anyone to perish. He wants everyone to wake up and come to him just as the Prodigal did to his father. This being so, the Spirit is working with everyone to bring about this wakefulness.

The Lord is not procrastinating concerning his promise [to return], as some count procrastination; but he is patient towards you, not wishing for any to perish, but that everyone would come to repentance. (2 Peter 3.9)

As we relate to all those persons whom we touch in life, we can be assured that they have already had some encounters with the presence of God in their lives. A better opening to our witness to others than, "Do you know that you are lost?" is for us to acknowledge that God is already moving and ask, "How are you and God doing?" This question respects the spiritual struggles of another, and also recognizes that God is moving in all of the lives of this world.

God is working behind the scenes of our lives

We should also be very aware that as we do what God wants us to do, we have a behind the scenes helper. God is there already working to secure his will. As we assist him with his work, he works with us to bring it about. We are never alone. We can never assume that what we can observe is all that is going on in any situation. We cannot see into the heart and spirit. We must simply believe that God is working just as we are working. We are in partnership with him as we go about his business. Jesus said:

And he said, "Whoever has ears to hear, let him hear." (Mark 4.9)

Not everyone can see the movement of God, and not everyone can hear the sound of his presence. Believers know by faith that he is there. Jesus said in the Great Commission, "Go and I am with you always…"

What is God doing with us?

If we are looking to detect the presence and actions of God around us, what are we expecting to see? Many things of course, but the biggest secret is found in the belief that God is a God of grace. As mentioned above in earlier chapters, grace is a gift, and it is not limited in its expression to those who deserve it. God gives gifts to everyone regardless of whether they deserve them.

So, in attempting to detect the moving presence of God around us we will be looking for the constant gifts of blessing that he is giving to us and to everyone else.

Every good gift and every perfect gift is from above, coming down from the Father of lights, with whom there is no variation or a constantly changing shadow. (James 1.17)

God is in the good gifting business. He is constantly gifting us all in good ways. But, can we detect those gifts? Usually persons are not believing that he is acting in this way, and they do not expect the gifts. Therefore, they do not have the eyes to see them nor ears to hear of them.

When we believe we can detect. When we do not know what he is doing, we are not prepared to be aware of his gifting. We only see what we believe will be.

12. The Peoples of the World Desperately Need the Message

"Therefore, go and make students of all peoples, immersing them in the name of the Father and the Son and the Holy Spirit, teaching them to practice all that I instructed you; and lo, I am with you always, even to the end of the age." (Jesus in Matthew 28.19-20)

Sanctify your hearts in the Lord Christ. Always be ready to give answers to everyone who asks you about the message of hope which is in you, with humility and reverence. (1 Peter 3.15)

It was not difficult for early Christians to talk about their belief in Jesus. After all, they were surrounded by people who believed in and served all kinds of bad news gods. They were living in a world in which the prevailing lifestyle was "dog eat dog" and "every man for himself."

There were good, decent, honest people in all places, but the ethic of most people was not based on the Ten Commandments or anything similar. It was a lawless world.

The people of God are strange in the world

After they came to believe in the teachings of Jesus about the person of God and the lifestyle that he lives and instructs us to live, they became strange people in every place in which they lived. To be gracious, forgiving, caring, and honest meant to be different.

Naturally, other people would want to know why they behaved as they did. Their curiosity opened all kinds of doors to share the good news revealed by Jesus. Christians had to be prepared to give good and accurate answers about their beliefs and lifestyle.

Also, the Good News was too good not to be known everywhere. God had broken into our world with his Son and revealed himself and his will in ways never imagined before. Jesus revealed him to be our heavenly Father rather some detached holy other. He revealed him to be a Father of grace and *agape*. God is sending his Spirit into the hearts and lives of all those who believe and is remaking them in his image with his personality. This was indeed a wonderful new vision of who God is and what he is about.

The message of Jesus is powerful

The Jesus message is so powerful that it facilitates changes in the
spirits and attitudes and lifestyles of those who accept it. It is magical in its life-changing power. Paul experienced this change in himself as he left his legalistic judgmentalism behind for the graciousness which he found in Jesus. He spent the rest of his life helping others to have a similar experience.

The spirit of grace and the lifestyle of grace is dramatic in its affects in daily living. When persons believe in it and live it, it changes them and their world.

Jesus talked about the creation of a new kingdom of people who were different from the rest of the world. His is a kingdom of the spirit rather than the body. It is not geographical, political, or racial. Its people become citizens because of what is inside of them rather than where they live or what their DNA. They share the same hope for new life, and for the lifestyle taught by their Lord.

Importantly, they wish that everyone might experience the same power as they. It is such wonderfully good news that it must be given as a gift to any who will listen. Real life is available to all. But, people cannot believe and receive it unless someone tells them the story. It is a great story and Christians must learn how to enjoy telling it.

The dead can live

"Truly, I say to you, he who accepts my teachings and believes that God sent me, has eternal life and is not in need of condemnation, but he has passed out of death into life. Truly, I say to you, the hour is coming, and now is, when the dead shall hear and understand the utterance of the Son of God: and they who receive it shall become alive." (Jesus in John 5.24-25)

The realization that persons are living dead lives is a motivation for us. Everyone may have life if they will believe and follow Jesus. The rich, young ruler had everything a person could wish for in worldly goods and recognition, but he was dead inside. Jesus showed him how to come to life, but he could not believe that it would work.

Paul was similar to that young ruler. He was a man of position and possessions, but he found a far better treasure on the Damascus Road. He found a heavenly life of gifting grace. He was never the same, and never wished to return to his old ways. He had found life.

Being a witness does not simple mean to be a "soul winner". It means learning how to share all aspects of the teachings of Jesus. When we share that God is a Heavenly Father of grace and graciousness, we are witnessing to the Good News. When we testify to the power of being a forgiving person, we are witnessing to the Good News. When we share the possibility of being immersed in the Spirit of God, we are witnessing to the Good News. All of the insights and lifestyle ways we have studied are part of the Good News. When we share any of them with other persons we are sharing the Good News.

We must learn to understand the ways in which God has given us life, and be able to share that change with those who do not yet know. This book is one way to share the message. It shares spirit and lifestyle. It illustrates the difference between just living and having life.

13. A Spirit of Joy is a Reconciler

We live in a world of estrangement. Persons are estranged from other persons. People groups are estranged from other peoples. Races are estranged. Religions are estranged from others. Nations are estranged.

Estrangement does not contribute to fullness of life. It dissipates life. It is caused by many things: differing opinions, past harm and hurt, misunderstanding and miscommunication, competing allegiances, fears, and a multitude of other problems. But, what can be done about such abiding and pervasive problems? Jesus taught that we should be reconcilers.

Reconciliation is all about relationships that are broken. It speaks to persons who are at odds with each other. This kind of estrangement is the seedbed from which multitudes of other problems grow. It is no wonder that Jesus addressed it in his teachings. At one time he placed reconciliation ahead of acts of worship.

"Therefore, if you are offering your gift at the altar, and while there remember that your brother has a grievance against you, leave your gift there before the altar, and go your way. Be reconciled to your brother first, and then come and offer your gift."
(Jesus in Matthew 5.23-24)

Broken relationships rob life of joy, and provide the opportunity to continually experience unhappiness. This is especially true when the persons involved are living life in close proximity to each other. The reason for the estrangement can be a constant source of continuing agitation.

The teaching above instructs us to correct actions we may have taken which have caused estrangement. It does not place on us the responsibility for solving the entire issue. We cannot. We are to behave in ways that do not contribute to estrangement, and when we cause it, to attempt to correct what we have done.

Most of these lifestyle ways taught by Jesus can be instrumental in repairing relationships. But they must be exercised by one who is seeking reconciliation. When they are lived out in that relationship, they can be the instruments of healing.

God sent Jesus to help with our reconciliation to him

In Jesus, the Father was taking the first step toward us to reconcile us to himself. God is a God of reconciliation and constantly takes steps to bring persons into close relationship with himself.

As is the case with all of these behavioral points, reconciliation is an activity of grace. It issues forth from a heart and spirit of grace. It is edifying, forgiving, peacemaking. It is a demonstration of grace in action. It is *agape*.

All of these things are from God, who has reconciled us to himself through Jesus Christ, and has given to us the ministry of reconciliation.

God was in Christ reconciling the world to himself, not charging them for their destructive living, and has committed to us the message of reconciliation. Therefore, we are ambassadors for Christ, as though God were encouraging you through us. We exhort you on Christ's behalf, be reconciled with God. (2 Corinthians 5.18-20)

You, who were in the past a stranger and hostile in your understanding and in destructive living, he has now reconciled, laying down his physical body in death, to present you holy and spotless and blameless before him. (Colossians 1.21-22)

Paul was keenly aware of the role he was playing in the work of God on Earth. He illustrates that understanding in these verses to the churches as he sees all of us partnering with the living God to save a world from itself. We live in a world of estrangement. Persons and nations are constantly at odds with each other. When estrangement is present, peace and joy are not. We have been called to work with the Father to restore peace and overcome estrangement. We are reconcilers as he is a reconciler.

14. Giving Joy to the Poor and Needy

Christians have always been known for their compassion for the poor and needy. Throughout history, they have ministered and created institutional ministries to help those who are unfortunate. They inherited this concern from the Jews who provided the framework for this new faith. The Jews were wonderfully caring for the poor. Jesus told Christians to continue with the same sensitivity.

"I was hungry, and you gave me something to eat. I was thirsty, and you gave me something to drink. I was a stranger, and you let me stay with you. Naked, and you clothed me. I was sick, and you came to see me. I was in prison, and you came to help me.
"Then shall the righteous answer him, saying, 'Lord, when did we find you hungry, and fed you, or thirsty, and gave you something to drink? When did we see you as a stranger, and let you stay with us, or naked, and gave you clothing? When did we see you sick, or in prison, and come to visit you?'
"And the King shall answer them, 'Truly I say to you, because you did it for one of these my brethren, even the least important of these, you did it for me.'"
(Jesus in Matthew 25.35-40)

The most obvious and easiest place in which believers may share their joy in the Lord is with those who are most needy. The needy have multitudes of places in their lives where joy can be applied. They offer immediate opportunities for results to been seen and experienced.

Jesus identified with their needs in the passage above. When we take joy to the needy, we take joy to the Lord himself. The joy idea infuses the situation with a wonderful possibility. When we focus on how to give joy rather than food, shelter, clothing, and so forth, we make our efforts more pointed. We actually want to create joy in a life that may have little joy because of overwhelming physical needs.

The goal does require us to seek to understand situations and what it may take to bring joy about. The first inclination may not be the best. When joy is our goal, we have not finished the task by simply giving food. We may discover that food is one of the lesser needs persons may have. We have to probe somewhat to find the more meaningful needs in a person's life.

However, this behavior needs to remain related to the basic human needs of persons. Others address spiritual and emotional needs. Our quest here is to discover and supply those needs to persons which are actually needs, the ones which bring joy to those receiving them. We succeed when we know that joy is taking place because of our efforts. We are blessing the people of our world.

Christians need to be proactive in making sure that ministry is an important part of their lives. The concern should not be occasional or hit and miss. Specific commitments should be made which keep us involved in helping on an ongoing basis.

A Message that Gives Life

The revelations that make up the Jesus message are revelations that change beliefs, understandings, mindset, values, and worldview. They give persons a fresh and different look at themselves, God, and how to go about daily living. These happenings cause life to change and become more than before. The message, when believed and practiced, causes persons to have life in ways not before experienced.

Life experiences peace and joy in abundance. It becomes an overflow of grace and graciousness. This kind of heavenly life lifts the spirit and causes the soul to sing. It is in sync with the Father and the Son. It is attended by angels who celebrate its existence.

The truth and spirit revealed by Jesus creates a people who become part of a kingdom of the spirit. This kingdom is not bound by geography or politics. It is a kingdom of people with a new and different spirit and lifestyle. It is bigger than any other kingdom on Earth.

Remarkably, the people of this kingdom can live within any political or religious environment. Since their kingdom is a kingdom of the spirit, the physical setting of their lives does not control that spirit. It is there and it is connected to the Living God no matter the world in which they live.

This kingdom of the spirit is not expressed by religious ceremony or participation. It is expressed in the personality and daily lifestyle of persons. It is not about religious expression. It is about belief and perception that lead to behavior. It is not about being religious. It is about being a person with the Spirit of God housed inside.

The message of Jesus results in the creation of new persons. It creates a new spirit within them. It creates a new lifestyle that is lived out by them. It is a new orientation. It produces a new perception of self, God, and others. Behold, all things become new!

"Truly, I say to you, he who hears my message, and believes it was [God] who sent me, has life of the heavens, and does not need condemnation, but has passed out of death into life." (Jesus in John 5.24)

"Therefore, go and make students of all peoples, immersing them in the name of the Father and the Son and the Holy Spirit, teaching them to practice all that I instructed you; and lo, I am with you always, even to the end of the age." (Jesus in Matthew 28.19-20)

Appendix 1
What is Sin?

Most religious people have well developed ideas about their understanding of sin. It is a major concern for many. But, what is it after all? What does the Christian New Testament identify as sin, and why?

A Definition

Sin is that which destroys life, spirit, and relationships in the life of persons. It may be understandings or actions. Its end result is the same: life is less because of it. The word "sin" means to miss the mark, be inaccurate to the truth, or to be erroneous as a lifestyle seeking the best and highest. Sin harms, destroys, misleads, and thwarts.

Religious people usually see sin as being against God, and they think that its bad results are rewards from God for disobedience. In fact, sin is sin whether one is religious or not. Sin is sin because of its destructive and debilitating results in spirit and life, not just because a religion says that it is wrong. Most negative results of sin are not the punishment of a god. They are the natural results of the sins themselves.

Societies identify sins that are important to themselves. Many do this in the name of their religion. But the sins identified are very similar from culture to culture and religion to religion. The Ten Commandments have never been unique to Judaism. They contain prohibitions common to all societies:

Do not murder
Do not steal
Do not falsely accuse another
Do not commit adultery
Do not envy

Societies have recognized the harmfulness of these kinds of lifestyles no matter what their religious observances. This is so because these behaviors are obviously detrimental to the social fabric of a person, tribe, town, or state.

How Do We Know What is Sin?

This is one of life's most vexing questions. Most people have their own lists, as do societies. But how do we really know what kinds of actions build life and what kinds destroy life?

The Garden of Eden story in the book of Genesis obviously predates the Hebrews and Judaism. Moses did not pen or compile the first five books of the Bible until 1400-1300 BCE. The Adam and Eve story had been passed down for generations before that. And that story deals with the secret of what is right and wrong. The fruit of the forbidden tree would give Adam and Eve the ability to distinguish between what is right for persons and what is wrong for persons. It is the common quest of all persons to try to understand which is which.

Jesus the Revealer of Right and Life

Jesus dealt with the issue of right and wrong when he taught,

Enter through the narrow gate. The gate is wide and the way is broad which leads to destruction, and there are many who enter through it. The gate is small and the way is narrow which leads to life, and there are few who find it. (Matthew 7.13-14)

His point is that the way is difficult to find. Where does one go to find the answers for happiness and fulfillment? Discovering that which is sinful and destructive is far easier than finding that which is fulfilling. Jesus went on to say that he had come to reveal the way,

The thief comes only to steal and kill and destroy; I came that they may have life, and have it overflowingly. (John 10.10)

The Garden of Eden account indicates that God knows the difference between right and wrong, but humans do not. It also implies that we must get such information from God if we are to know it. He is our source. He speaks to humanity through revelations to persons who speak for him to the world. These persons have been called angels and prophets, because they speak a message from God. Jesus said that he was such a messenger,

"Truly, I say to you, he who hears my message, and believes it was him who sent me, has life of the heavens, and does not need condemnation, but has passed out of death into life." (John 5.24)

The writer of Hebrews said,

God, after he spoke long ago to the fathers through the prophets in many fragments and in many ways, in these last days has spoken to us through his Son, whom he appointed the recipient of all things, through whom also he made the age. (Hebrews 1.1-2)

Jesus Discounted Religious Taboos as Being Sinful

The religious world of Israel into which Jesus came, was riddled with religious taboos that were labeled as sin. Jewish scholars had for several centuries continued to spin out applications of the Ten Commandments and Levitical laws. Each Commandment was further and further defined in great detail to state what actions are a violation of its intent. Jesus was constantly running into specifics about what could not be done on the Sabbath in order to preserve its holiness.

At that time Jesus went through the grain fields on the Sabbath, and his disciples became hungry and began to pick the heads of grain and eat them. But when the Pharisees saw this, they said to him, "Look, your disciples are doing what is not lawful to do on a Sabbath." (Matthew 12.1-2)

A man was there whose hand was withered.
They questioned Jesus, asking, "Is it lawful to heal on
the Sabbath?"--so that they might accuse him. And he
said to them, "What man is there among you who has
a sheep, and if it falls into a pit on the Sabbath, will he
not take hold of it and lift it out?" (Matthew 12.10-11)

Immediately the man became well, and picked
up his pallet and began to walk. Now it was the
Sabbath on that day. So the Judeans were saying to
the man who was cured, "It is the Sabbath, and it is
not permissible for you to carry your pallet." (John
5.9-10)

Jesus indicated that the Ten Commandments
had been misunderstood by the rabbis. They were not
intended to be a burden around the necks of the
people. They were intended to help persons know how
to live life at its best.

Jesus said to them, "The Sabbath was made for
man, and not man for the Sabbath." (Mark 2.27)

Jewish purification laws were also disrespected
by Jesus. He did not honor rules and prohibitions that
prevented persons from being the kind of persons
whom God desired. The Parable of the Good
Samaritan is an example in which purification laws
kept a priest and a Levite from helping a man in need,
while a despised Samaritan helped in spite of them.

"And by chance a priest was going down on that road, and when he saw him, he passed by over on the other side of the road. In a similar manner a Levite, when he came to the place and saw him, passed by on the other side." (Luke 10.31-32)

It is probable that the reason the two professional religious men did not help the man is because they could be made ritually unclean by touching blood or a dead body. Their religious taboos were more important than the man who needed desperate assistance. By telling this story as he did, Jesus identified what is important to God and what is not.

The many minor legalisms of religion are not important to God. That which is sin is that which actually does harm to persons and to society.

New Testament Uses for the Word Sin

In the New Testament, the Greek word *hamartia* is commonly used, but in various ways, all of which are translated into English as "sin." The Greek word *parabasis* is usually translated as "disobedience" or "transgression." The root meaning of *hamartia* was to miss an intended mark, or to be wrong or in error.

Sin as a transgression of the Ten Commandments: The woman caught in adultery.

Sin as a violation of Jewish mini laws: The sinners with whom Jesus dined were called sinners because they did not observe the hundreds of mini laws that grew out of the Ten Commandments.

Sin as an error: Jesus used the word to mean an error in understanding.

> *Yet because I tell the truth, you do not believe me! Can any of you prove me guilty of error? If I am telling the truth, why don't you believe me?* (John 8.45-46 NIV)

Sin as thinking wrongly

> *"Why do you not understand what I am saying? It is because you cannot understand my message. You are of your father the devil, and you want to do the passions of your father. He was a murderer from the beginning and does not stand in the truth because there is no truth in him. Whenever he tells a lie, he speaks from his own nature, because he is a liar and the father of lies. But because I speak the truth, you do not believe me."* (John 8.43-45)

Since *hamartia* is used in various ways in the New Testament, it is not always easy to tell exactly how to translate it into English. The context in which it is used is the best indication of its meaning. And, even then the translation may be debatable. For instance,

> *in these last days [God] has spoken to us in his Son, whom he appointed the recipient of all things,*

through whom also he made the age. And he is the brightness of his glory and the exact representation of his personality, and supports everything in his message by his power. When he had cleansed us of missing the mark, he sat down at the right hand of the Majesty on high, (Hebrews 1.2-3)

The translation, "purification of sins," is a strange one for the context of this paragraph. The context is about Jesus revealing the person and character of God through his own person and through his message. The implication being that the world does not know who God really is and what he is really about. Jesus has come to set the record straight. He used the cleansing idea in explaining the power of his revelations.

"You are already clean because of the message I have spoken to you." (John 15.3)

"Make them godly by means of the truth; your message is truth." (John 17.17)

so that He might make her godly, having cleansed her like a washing with water, by means of the message, (Ephesians 5.26)

In that context, the use of *hamartia* must have more to do with misunderstanding and error in understanding than about overt transgressions. Jesus is communicating the truth about the Father in order to offset the misunderstandings that exist. So, *hamartia* should more accurately be translated "misunderstandings." The verse would then read, "when he had cleansed us of our misunderstandings." This translation would be more in keeping with the context of the passage.

Because translators believe the mission of Jesus was primarily about sacrificing himself for the sins of mankind, they are prone to translate everything related to purification and sin as part of that sacrificial process. In the case above, the context indicates that the subject is really Jesus' revelation of the Father. The purification or cleansing being accomplished is a cleansing of the mind and beliefs rather than that of behavioral transgressions.

It is easy to mistranslate words from one language to another. Numerous renderings are possible and the translator usually uses the one most appealing to himself. Sometimes this can be a mistranslation.

The meaning of sin is always about that which is erroneous whether it be actions done or a mindset which is wrong. Jesus came to help us with both because both rob life of its fullness and joy. That is why sin is sin. It destroys life and causes the death of the spirit.

Jesus did not seem to take sin personally

We tend to think of sin as a personal affront to God, and that he reacts to our sin as though it is a personal attack on his will. Jesus did not give that impression at all. He showed us that God does not react to sin in that way.

Jesus acted almost as though he were a third party observing the problems of those around him. They were struggling with sin in their lives, but their sin was not an affront to him. The most powerful example is his prayer on the cross for God to forgive those who were crucifying him because they did not know what they were doing. As personal as his crucifixion was to him, he did not take their actions as a personal affront. They were slaves to sin and knew no better.

If Jesus were accurately demonstrating the attitude of God toward our sin, then we can see the truth in his portrait of the father of the Prodigal Son. The young man had destroyed his own life and squandered his inheritance, but his father did not act as though he were affronted by what the son had done. He wanted the best for his son and rejoiced that he had come to his senses. What the son had done did not change his relationship to the son.

This parable flew in the face of all of the legalistic understandings of the scribes and Pharisees. It revealed God to be someone entirely different than they understood. His hate for our sinfulness was an important factor in their theological understandings. They thought that God hates sin and sinners so much that he cannot have either in his presence. Jesus revealed God to be very different than that.

The reason God could be like the father of the Prodigal is that he is an observer of our plight with sin and not a participant. He does not take our sinfulness personally. Sin is sin. It kills and destroys by its very nature. God does not have to do the rewarding for sinfulness. Sin carries its own destructive results. Punishment for sin takes place by its very nature without God having to act to see that it does.

Jesus understood this truth about sin and pitied those enslaved by sinful understandings and behavior. He came to set us free from its power. His message is the instrument for giving us that freedom.

Appendix 2
Trespasses and Sins

He has brought life to you who were dead in
trespasses and sins; (Ephesians 2.1)

English Translators Often Miss the Point

Translators of the English New Testament have
had difficulty in capturing the original meanings of
numerous Greek words and concepts. They have
sought to be accurate in the translation of the original
narratives, but constantly search for English concepts
that accurately convey biblical meanings. Their job is
not easy by any means. Words can be very difficult to
understand in biblical passages that are filled with
symbolism and special meaning.

The meanings of "trespasses" and "sins" are a
good example of the problem. Normal understandings
of these two words are that they are almost the same in
meaning. They are understood to mean immoral,
unethical, or ungodly thoughts and actions. The
emphasis is on bad behavior. It is behavior that is
unpleasing to God, and carries guilt that must be
satisfied lest God punish its perpetrator.

Trespasses and Transgressions

Actually, the two words are different in the
original Greek language. The word *parapatoma* in

Greek actually means behavior that is against the rules of God when used by Pharisees and lawyers. It is accurately translated as "transgression" or "trespass."

It may also mean to "miss the mark" in that it defines behavior that is off target. In this case, the target is righteousness or the commandments of God. But it also generally means to be off line in pursuing a full and rewarding life.

The Jewish faith believed that it possessed the lifestyle of God, and that lifestyle produced the most full and satisfying life on Earth. It was given to Moses by God on the Mountain and therefore was "eternal" or "heavenly" life. It was God's kind of life. It was life like that in the heavens. If one violated the laws of Moses, he was missing the mark. He was off track in being rewarded with fullness of life from God.

Sins Are More Ambiguous

The Greek word *hamartia* is almost universally translated as "sin." Sin is an ancient English word that carries a concept of guilt. It is primarily a religious word that refers to any behavior that displeases the deity.

The Greeks, however, had several meanings for *hamartia* in their language. It could be translated as "wrong", "error", "mistake" or any number of other words that convey the meaning of being off base in thinking or acting. Additionally, the word carried a concept of wrong thinking or acting in ways that bring bad results.

When English translators choose to use "sin" alone as a proper translation of *hamartia*, they are obscuring the actual meaning of a Scripture passage. The context in which *hamartia* is found determines the English meaning of the word for the writer using it. When translators ignore context in favor of a single word in English, "sin", meanings are lost. This can lead to tragic results.

The Plural Has Special Meaning

The plural of *hamartia* is used early in the New Testament to indicate behaviors which lead to punishment from God and reversals in life. Later, as the message of Jesus is understood and experienced, the plural form, "sins" often relates to the misunderstandings of God held by people in general. This is seen in a graphic way in John 8.30ff.

John relates a conversation between Jesus and his Judean followers about their misunderstandings of God and his will. Jesus states that they have been deceived by the Adversary to the extent that they cannot accept the truth when they hear it. In essence, they have been "brainwashed" by lies. He challenges them to convict him of any such "error" (sin).

The passage is all about truth and lies. To understand the subject to be immorality or lawlessness is to miss the context. Jesus is addressing their misunderstandings. They understand God wrongly. They wrongly understand God's will for them. They misunderstand what God is trying to do with them. They are bound up in misconceptions. To translate *hamartia* as "sin" in these passages is to miss the message.

Many verses in the New Testament use *hamartia* in this way, as a blindness to the truth about God. It is no wonder that another key Greek word used in the NT is also translated wrongly. It relates to *hamartia*. It is *metanoia* and is usually translated as "repent." If one believes that *hamartia* means sin, then it is easy to see why *metanoia* means to repent of sin.

Sin and Repentance

The Greek word, *metanoia*, actually means to "change one's mind or thinking." When we see that "sins" usually referred to wrong thinking and understanding about God and his will, we can also see why it was important to change that thinking and understanding. "Repentance" does not do justice to *metanoia*. Repentance means to "be sorry for wrongdoing," while *metanoia* means to change one's thinking. These are two entirely different experiences.

Jesus often spoke of his "Word." Although the Greek word here is *logos*, it also has several meanings when being translated. Here Jesus was obviously referring to his message. That message was the content of his revelation about God and life in God. When one receives the message of Jesus, the possibility for a new spirit and life becomes real. (John 5.24-25) But it cannot have any affect in a person unless that person is willing to change his thinking and understanding. Without a willingness to change thinking, release from the lies of the past is not possible. (Luke 24.47)

Paul summed this up in his letter to the Roman Christians when he talked about becoming transformed,

Do not be conformed to this world, but be transformed by the renewing of your thinking. Then you will be able to demonstrate the good, acceptable and complete will of God. (Romans 12.2)

The revelations of Jesus were light to mankind that leads to life. They issue forth in an acceptance of a new spirit and lifestyle.

John the Baptist said that Jesus would immerse people in a new spirit, the spirit of God.

"I did not recognize him, but he who sent me to immerse in water said to me, 'He upon whom you see the Spirit descending and remaining upon him, this is the one who immerses in the Holy Spirit.'" (John 1.33)

This new spirit is a product of the message of Jesus. When persons realize what Jesus has been revealing and teaching them, they become possessed of a new understanding and new spirit. They begin to understand grace and the spirit of grace. The understanding changes their thinking and changes their lives. They become free from the "sins" which had enslaved their thinking and behaving. They are no longer the products of this world. They have been born from above, born again. They were dead in sins and trespasses. Now, they are becoming alive.